EARLY WELSH HISTORIES

EARLY WELSH HISTORIES

GILDAS AND NENNIUS

Translated by J. A. Giles

Cockatrice Books
Y diawl a'm llaw chwith

Translations of Gildas, *De Excidio et Conquestu Britanniae* and Nennius, *Historia Brittonum* by J. A. Giles (1808–1884) first appeared in *The Works of Gildas and Nennius* (London: James Bohn, 1841).

This edition copyright © Cockatrice Books, 2020
www.cockatrice-books.com
mail@cockatrice-books.com

All rights reserved. No part of this publication may be reproduced, stored in a retrieval system or transmitted in any form or by any means, electronic, mechanical, photocopying, recording or otherwise, without prior permission of the publisher.

Cover image by 'sbuwert' taken from Adobe Stock Images: carvings on a Pictish stone.

Published as part of the Wales in Europe series, celebrating the past and future of Wales as an independent nation.

CONTENTS

GILDAS
ON THE RUIN OF BRITAIN 7
I. The Preface 7
II. The History 15

NENNIUS
THE HISTORY OF THE BRITONS 44
I. The Prologue 44
II. The Apology of Nennius 47
III. The History 48
The Genealogy of the Kings of Bernicia. 103
The Genealogy Of The Kings Of Kent 104
The Origin Of The Kings Of East-Anglia 104
The Genealogy Of The Mercians 105
The Kings of the Deiri 105

GILDAS
ON THE RUIN OF BRITAIN

I. The Preface

1. Whatever in this my epistle I may write in my humble but well meaning manner, rather by way of lamentation than for display, let no one suppose that it springs from contempt of others or that I foolishly esteem myself as better than they; for alas! the subject of my complaint is the general destruction of every thing that is good, and the general growth of evil throughout the land; — but that I rejoice to see her revive therefrom: for it is my present purpose to relate the deeds of an indolent and slothful race, rather than the exploits of those who have been valiant in the field.* I have kept silence, I confess, with

---

* Notwithstanding this remark of Gildas, the Britons must have shown great bravery and resolution in their battles

much mental anguish, compunction of feeling and contrition of heart, whilst I revolved all these things within myself; and, as God the searcher of the reins is witness, for the space of even ten years or more, my inexperience, as at present also, and my unworthiness preventing me from taking upon myself the character of a censor. But I read how the illustrious lawgiver, for one word's doubting, was not allowed to enter the desired land; that the sons of the high-priest, for placing strange fire upon God's altar, were cut off by a speedy death; that God's people, for breaking the law of God, save two only, were slain by wild beasts, by fire and sword in the deserts of Arabia, though God had so loved them that he had made a way for them through the Red Sea, had fed them with bread from heaven, and water from the rock, and by the lifting up of a hand merely had made their armies invincible; and then, when they had crossed the Jordan and entered the unknown land, and the walls of the city had fallen down flat at the sound only of a

> against the Saxons, or they would not have resisted their encroachments so long. When Gildas was writing, a hundred years had elapsed, and the Britons still possessed a large portion of their native country.

trumpet, the taking of a cloak and a little gold from the accursed things caused the deaths of many: and again the breach of their treaty with the Gibeonites, though that treaty had been obtained by fraud, brought destruction upon many; and I took warning from the sins of the people which called down upon them the reprehensions of the prophets and also of Jeremiah, with his fourfold Lamentations written in alphabetical order. I saw moreover in my own time, as that prophet also had complained, that the city had sat down lone and widowed, which before was full of people; that the queen of nations and the princess of provinces (i.e. the church), had been made tributary; that the gold was obscured, and the most excellent colour (which is the brightness of God's word) changed; that the sons of Sion (i.e. of holy mother church), once famous and clothed in the finest gold, grovelled in dung; and what added intolerably to the weight of grief of that illustrious man, and to mine, though but an abject, whilst he had thus mourned them in their happy and prosperous condition, 'Her Nazarites were fairer than snow, more ruddy than old ivory, more beautiful than the sapphire.' These and many other passages in the ancient Scriptures I regarded as a kind of mirror of human life, and I turned also to the New, wherein I read more clearly what perhaps to me before was dark, for the darkness fled, and truth shed her steady light — I read therein that the Lord had said, 'I came not but to the lost sheep of the house of Israel;' and on the other hand, 'But the children of this kingdom shall be cast out into outer darkness; there shall be weeping and gnashing of teeth:' and again, 'It is not good to take the children's meat and to give it to dogs:' also, 'Woe to you, scribes and Pharisees, hypocrites!' I heard how 'many shall come from the east and the west and shall sit down with Abraham, Isaac, and Jacob in the kingdom of heaven:' and on the contrary, 'I will then say to them "Depart from me, ye workers of iniquity!"' I read, 'Blessed are the barren and the teats which have not given suck;' and on the contrary, 'Those, who were ready, entered with him to the wedding; afterwards came the other virgins also, saying "Lord, Lord, open to us:" to whom it was answered, "I do not know you."' I heard, forsooth, 'Whoever shall believe and be baptized, shall be saved, but whoever shall not believe shall be damned.' I read in the words of the apostle that the branch of the wild olive was grafted upon the good olive, but should nevertheless be cut off from the communion of the root of its fatness, if it did not hold itself in fear, but entertained lofty thoughts. I knew the mercy of the Lord, but I also feared his judgment: I praised his grace, but I feared the rendering to every man according to his works: perceiving the sheep of the same fold to be different, I deservedly commended Peter for his entire confession of Christ, but called Judas most wretched, for his love of covetousness: I thought Stephen most glorious on account of the palm of martyrdom, but Nicholas wretched for his mark of unclean heresy: I read assuredly, 'They had all things common:' but likewise also, as it is written, 'Why have ye conspired to tempt the Spirit of God?' I saw, on the other hand, how much security had grown upon the men of our time, as if there were nothing to cause them fear. These things, therefore, and many more which for brevity's sake we have determined to omit, I revolved again and again in my amazed mind with compunction in my heart, and I thought to myself, 'If God's peculiar people, chosen from all the people of the world, the royal seed, and holy nation, to whom he had said, "My first begotten Israel," its priests, prophets, and kings, throughout so many ages, his servant and apostle, and the members of his primitive church, were not spared when they deviated from the right path, what will he do to the darkness of this our age, in which, besides all the huge and heinous sins, which it has common with all the wicked of the world committed, is found an innate, indelible, and irremediable load of folly and inconstancy?' 'What, wretched man (I say to myself) is it given to you, as if you were an illustrious and learned teacher, to oppose the force of so violent a torrent, and keep the charge committed to you against such a series of inveterate crimes which has spread far and wide, without interruption, for so many years? Hold thy peace: to do otherwise, is to tell the foot to see, and the hand to speak. Britain has rulers, and she has watchmen: why dost thou incline thyself thus uselessly to prate?' She has such, I say, not too many, perhaps, but surely not too few: but, because they are bent down and pressed beneath so heavy a burden, they have not time allowed them to take breath. My senses, therefore, as if feeling a portion of my debt and obligation, preoccupied themselves with such objections, and with others yet more strong. They struggled, as I said, no short time, in fearful strait, whilst I read, 'There is a time for speaking, and a time for keeping silence.' At length, the creditor's side prevailed and bore off the victory: if (said he) thou art not bold enough to be marked with the comely mark of golden liberty among the prophetic creatures, who enjoy the rank as reasoning beings next to the angels, refuse not the inspiration of the understanding ass, to that day dumb, which would not carry forward the tiara'd magician who was going to curse God's people, but in the narrow pass of the vineyard crushed his loosened foot, and thereby felt the lash; and though he was, with his ungrateful and furious hand, against right justice, beating her innocent sides, she pointed out to him the heavenly messenger holding the naked sword, and standing in his way, though he had not seen him.

Wherefore in zeal for the house of God and for his holy law, constrained either by the reasonings of my own thoughts, or by the pious entreaties of my brethren, I now discharge the debt so long exacted of me; humble, indeed, in style, but faithful, as I think, and friendly to all Christ's youthful soldiers, but severe and insupportable to foolish apostates; the former of whom, if I am not deceived, will receive the same with tears flowing from God's love; but the others with sorrow, such as is extorted from the indignation and pusillanimity of a convicted conscience.

2. I will, therefore, if God be willing, endeavour to say a few words about the situation of Britain, her disobedience and subjection, her rebellion, second subjection and dreadful slavery — of her religion, persecution, holy martyrs, heresies of different kinds — of her tyrants, her two hostile and ravaging nations — of her first devastation, her defence, her second devastation, and second taking vengeance — of her third devastation, of her famine, and the letters to Agitius* — of her victory and her crimes — of the sudden rumour of enemies — of her famous pestilence — of her counsels — of her last enemy, far more cruel than the first — of the subversion of her cities, and of the remnant that escaped; and finally, of the

---

* Or Aetius.

peace which, by the will of God, has been granted her in these our times.

II. The History

3. The island of Britain, situated on almost the utmost border of the earth, towards the south and west, and poised in the divine balance, as it is said, which supports the whole world, stretches out from the south-west towards the north pole, and is eight hundred miles long and two hundred broad,* except where the headlands of sundry promontories stretch farther into the sea. It is surrounded by the ocean, which forms winding bays, and is strongly defended by this ample, and, if I may so call it, impassable barrier, save on the south side, where the narrow sea affords a passage to Belgic Gaul. It is enriched by the mouths of two noble rivers, the Thames and the Severn, as it were two arms, by which foreign luxuries were of old imported, and by other streams of less importance. It is famous for eight

---

* The description of Britain is given in very nearly the same terms, by Orosius, Bede, and others, but the numbers denoting the length and breadth and other dimensions, are different in almost every MS. copy.

and twenty cities, and is embellished by certain castles, with walls, towers, well barred gates, and houses with threatening battlements built on high, and provided with all requisite instruments of defence. Its plains are spacious, its hills are pleasantly situated, adapted for superior tillage, and its mountains are admirably calculated for the alternate pasturage of cattle, where flowers of various colours, trodden by the feet of man, give it the appearance of a lovely picture. It is decked, like a man's chosen bride, with divers jewels, with lucid fountains and abundant brooks wandering over the snow white sands; with transparent rivers, flowing in gentle murmurs, and offering a sweet pledge of slumber* to those who recline upon their banks, whilst it is irrigated by abundant lakes, which pour forth cool torrents of refreshing water.

4. This island, stiff-necked and stubborn-minded, from the time of its being first inhabited, ungratefully rebels, sometimes against God, sometimes against her own citizens, and

---

* 'Soporem' in some MSS., 'saporem' in others; it is difficult from the turgidity and superabundance of the style to determine which is the best meaning.

frequently also, against foreign kings and their subjects. For what can there either be, or be committed, more disgraceful or more unrighteous in human affairs, than to refuse to show fear to God or affection to one's own countrymen, and (without detriment to one's faith) to refuse due honour to those of higher dignity, to cast off all regard to reason, human and divine, and, in contempt of heaven and earth, to be guided by one's own sensual inventions? I shall, therefore, omit those ancient errors common to all the nations of the earth, in which, before Christ came in the flesh, all mankind were bound; nor shall I enumerate those diabolical idols of my country, which almost surpassed in number those of Egypt, and of which we still see some mouldering away within or without the deserted temples, with stiff and deformed features as was customary. Nor will I call out upon the mountains, fountains, or hills, or upon the rivers, which now are subservient to the use of men, but once were an abomination and destruction to them, and to which the blind people paid divine honour. I shall also pass over the bygone times of our cruel tyrants, whose notoriety was spread over to far distant countries; so that Porphyry, that dog who in the east was always so fierce against the church, in his mad and vain style added this also, that 'Britain is a land fertile in tyrants.'* I will only endeavour to relate the evils which Britain suffered in the times of the Roman emperors, and also those which she caused to distant states; but so far as lies in my power, I shall not follow the writings and records of my own country, which (if there ever were any of them) have been consumed in the fires of the enemy, or have accompanied my exiled countrymen into distant lands, but be guided by the relations of foreign writers, which, being broken and interrupted in many places are therefore by no means clear.

5. For when the rulers of Rome had obtained the empire of the world, subdued all the neighbouring nations and islands towards the east, and strengthened their renown by the first peace which they made with the Parthians, who border on India, there was a general cessation from war throughout the whole world; the fierce

* Gildas here confuses the modern idea of a tyrant with that of an usurper. The latter is a sense in which Britain was said to be fertile in tyrants, viz. In usurpers of the imperial dignity.

flame which they kindled could not be extinguished or checked by the Western Ocean, but passing beyond the sea, imposed submission upon our island without resistance, and entirely reduced to obedience its unwarlike but faithless people, not so much by fire and sword and warlike engines, like other nations, but threats alone, and menaces of judgments frowning on their countenance, whilst terror penetrated to their hearts.

6. When afterwards they returned to Rome, for want of pay, as is said, and had no suspicion of an approaching rebellion, that deceitful lioness (Boadicea) put to death the rulers who had been left among them, to unfold more fully and to confirm the enterprises of the Romans. When the report of these things reached the senate, and they with a speedy army made haste to take vengeance on the crafty foxes,* as they called them, there was no bold navy on the sea to fight bravely for the country; by land there was no marshalled army, no right wing of battle, nor

---

* The Britons who fought under Boadicea were anything but 'crafty foxes.' 'Bold lions' is a much more appropriate appellation; they would also have been victorious if they had half the military advantages of the Romans.

other preparation for resistance; but their backs were their shields against their vanquishers, and they presented their necks to their swords, whilst chill terror ran through every limb, and they stretched out their hands to be bound, like women; so that it has become a proverb far and wide, that the Britons are neither brave in war nor faithful in time of peace.

7. The Romans, therefore, having slain many of the rebels, and reserved others for slaves, that the land might not be entirely reduced to desolation, left the island, destitute as it was of wine and oil, and returned to Italy, leaving behind them taskmasters, to scourge the shoulders of the natives, to reduce their necks to the yoke, and their soil to the vassalage of a Roman province; to chastise the crafty race, not with warlike weapons, but with rods, and if necessary to gird upon their sides the naked sword, so that it was no longer thought to be Britain, but a Roman island; and all their money, whether of copper, gold, or silver, was stamped with Caesar's image.

8. Meanwhile these islands, stiff with cold and frost, and in a distant region of the world, remote

from the visible sun, received the beams of light, that is, the holy precepts of Christ, the true Sun, showing to the whole world his splendour, not only from the temporal firmament, but from the height of heaven, which surpasses every thing temporal, at the latter part, as we know, of the reign of Tiberius Caesar, by whom his religion was propagated without impediment, and death threatened to those who interfered with its professors.

9. These rays of light were received with lukewarm minds by the inhabitants, but they nevertheless took root among some of them in a greater or less degree, until the nine years' persecution of the tyrant Diocletian, when the churches throughout the whole world were overthrown, all the copies of the Holy Scriptures which could be found burned in the streets, and the chosen pastors of God's flock butchered, together with their innocent sheep, in order that not a vestige, if possible, might remain in some provinces of Christ's religion. What disgraceful flights then took place — what slaughter and death inflicted by way of punishment in divers shapes, — what dreadful apostasies from religion;

and on the contrary, what glorious crowns of martyrdom then were won, — what raving fury was displayed by the persecutors, and patience on the part of the suffering saints, ecclesiastical history informs us; for the whole church were crowding in a body, to leave behind them the dark things of this world, and to make the best of their way to the happy mansions of heaven, as if to their proper home.

10. God, therefore, who wishes all men to be saved, and who calls sinners no less than those who think themselves righteous, magnified his mercy towards us, and, as we know, during the above-named persecution, that Britain might not totally be enveloped in the dark shades of night, he, of his own free gift, kindled up among us bright luminaries of holy martyrs, whose places of burial and of martyrdom, had they not for our manifold crimes been interfered with and destroyed by the barbarians, would have still kindled in the minds of the beholders no small fire of divine charity. Such were St. Alban of Verulam, Aaron and Julius, citizens of Carlisle,* and the rest, of both sexes, who in different

---

* Or Caerleon.

places stood their ground in the Christian contest.

11. The first of these martyrs, St. Alban, for charity's sake saved another confessor who was pursued by his persecutors, and was on the point of being seized, by hiding him in his house, and then by changing clothes with him, imitating in this example of Christ, who laid down his life for his sheep, and exposing himself in the other's clothes to be pursued in his stead. So pleasing to God was this conduct, that between his confession and martyrdom, he was honoured with the performance of wonderful miracles in presence of the impious blasphemers who were carrying the Roman standards, and like the Israelites of old, who trod dry-foot an unfrequented path whilst the ark of the covenant stood some time on the sands in the midst of Jordan; so also the martyr, with a thousand others, opened a path across the noble river Thames, whose waters stood abrupt like precipices on either side; and seeing this, the first of his executors was stricken with awe, and from a wolf became a lamb; so that he thirsted for martyrdom, and boldly underwent that for which

he thirsted. The other holy martyrs were tormented with divers sufferings, and their limbs were racked in such unheard of ways, that they, without delay, erected the trophies of their glorious martyrdom even in the gates of the city of Jerusalem. For those who survived, hid themselves in woods and deserts, and secret caves, waiting until God, who is the righteous judge of all, should reward their persecutors with judgment, and themselves with protection of their lives.

12. In less than ten years, therefore, of the above-named persecution, and when these bloody decrees began to fail in consequence of the death of their authors, all Christ's young disciples, after so long and wintry a night, begin to behold the genial light of heaven. They rebuild the churches, which had been levelled to the ground; they found, erect, and finish churches to the holy martyrs, and everywhere show their ensigns as token of their victory; festivals are celebrated and sacraments received with clean hearts and lips, and all the church's sons rejoice as it were in the fostering bosom of a mother. For this holy union remained between Christ their head and

the members of his church, until the Arian treason, fatal as a serpent, and vomiting its poison from beyond the sea, caused deadly dissension between brothers inhabiting the same house, and thus, as if a road were made across the sea, like wild beasts of all descriptions, and darting the poison of every heresy from their jaws, they inflicted dreadful wounds upon their country, which is ever desirous to hear something new, and remains constant long to nothing.

13. At length also, new races of tyrants sprang up, in terrific numbers, and the island, still bearing its Roman name, but casting off her institutes and laws, sent forth among the Gauls that bitter scion of her own planting Maximus, with a great number of followers, and the ensigns of royalty, which he bore without decency and without lawful right, but in a tyrannical manner, and amid the disturbances of the seditious soldiery. He, by cunning arts rather than by valour, attaching to his rule, by perjury and falsehood, all the neighbouring towns and provinces, against the Roman state, extended one of his wings to Spain, the other to Italy, fixed the seat

of his unholy government at Treves, and so furiously pushed his rebellion against his lawful emperors that he drove one of them out of Rome, and caused the other to terminate his most holy life. Trusting to these successful attempts, he not long after lost his accursed head before the walls of Aquileia, whereas he had before cut off the crowned heads of almost all the world.

14. After this, Britain is left deprived of all her soldiery and armed bands, of her cruel governors, and of the flower of her youth, who went with Maximus, but never again returned; and utterly ignorant as she was of the art of war, groaned in amazement for many years under the cruelty of two foreign nations — the Scots from the north-west, and the Picts from the north.

15. The Britons, impatient at the assaults of the Scots and Picts, their hostilities and dreadful oppressions, send ambassadors to Rome with letters, entreating in piteous terms the assistance of an armed band to protect them, and offering loyal and ready submission to the authority of Rome, if they only would expel their foes. A legion is immediately sent, forgetting their past rebellion, and provided sufficiently with arms.

When they had crossed over the sea and landed, they came at once to close conflict with their cruel enemies, and slew great numbers of them. All of them were driven beyond the borders, and the humiliated natives rescued from the bloody slavery which awaited them. By the advice of their protectors, they now built a wall across the island from one sea to the other, which being manned with a proper force, might be a terror to the foes whom it was intended to repel, and a protection to their friends whom it covered. But this wall, being made of turf instead of stone, was of no use to that foolish people, who had no head to guide them.

16. The Roman legion had no sooner returned home in joy and triumph, than their former foes, like hungry and ravening wolves, rushing with greedy jaws upon the fold which is left without a shepherd, and wafted both by the strength of oarsmen and the blowing wind, break through the boundaries, and spread slaughter on every side, and like mowers cutting down the ripe corn, they cut up, tread under foot, and overrun the whole country.

17. And now again they send suppliant ambassadors, with their garments rent and their heads covered with ashes, imploring assistance from the Romans, and like timorous chickens, crowding under the protecting wings of their parents, that their wretched country might not altogether be destroyed, and that the Roman name, which now was but an empty sound to fill the ear, might not become a reproach even to distant nations. Upon this, the Romans, moved with compassion, as far as human nature can be, at the relations of such horrors, send forward, like eagles in their flight, their unexpected bands of cavalry by land and mariners by sea, and planting their terrible swords upon the shoulders of their enemies, they mow them down like leaves which fall at the destined period; and as a mountain-torrent swelled with numerous streams, and bursting its banks with roaring noise, with foaming crest and yeasty wave rising to the stars, by whose eddying currents our eyes are as it were dazzled, does with one of its billows overwhelm every obstacle in its way, so did our illustrious defenders vigorously drive our enemies' band beyond the sea, if any could so escape them; for it was beyond those same seas

that they transported, year after year, the plunder which they had gained, no one daring to resist them.

18. The Romans, therefore, left the country, giving notice that they could no longer be harassed by such laborious expeditions, nor suffer the Roman standards, with so large and brave an army, to be worn out by sea and land by fighting against these unwarlike, plundering vagabonds; but that the islanders, inuring themselves to warlike weapons, and bravely fighting, should valiantly protect their country, their property, wives and children, and, what is dearer than these, their liberty and lives; that they should not suffer their hands to be tied behind their backs by a nation which, unless they were enervated by idleness and sloth, was not more powerful than themselves, but that they should arm those hands with buckler, sword, and spear, ready for the field of battle; and, because they thought this also of advantage to the people they were about to leave, they, with the help of the miserable natives, built a wall different from the former, by public and private contributions, and of the same structure as walls generally,

extending in a straight line from sea to sea, between some cities, which, from fear of their enemies, had there by chance been built. They then give energetic counsel to the timorous natives, and leave them patterns by which to manufacture arms. Moreover, on the south coast where their vessels lay, as there was some apprehension lest the barbarians might land, they erected towers at stated intervals, commanding a prospect of the sea; and then left the island never to return.

19. No sooner were they gone, than the Picts and Scots, like worms which in the heat of the mid-day come forth from their holes, hastily land again from their canoes, in which they had been carried beyond the Cichican* valley, differing one from another in manners, but inspired with the same avidity for blood, and all more eager to shroud their villainous faces in bushy hair than to cover with decent clothing those parts of their body which required it. Moreover, having heard of the departure of our friends, and their resolution never to return, they seized with

---

* The meaning of this expression is not known. O'Connor thinks it is the Irish Sea.

greater boldness than before on all the country towards the extreme north as far as the wall. To oppose them there was placed on the heights a garrison equally slow to fight and ill adapted to run away, a useless and panic-struck company, who slumbered away days and nights on their unprofitable watch. Meanwhile the hooked weapons of their enemies were not idle, and our wretched countrymen were dragged from the wall and dashed against the ground. Such premature death, however, painful as it was, saved them from seeing the miserable sufferings of their brothers and children. But why should I say more? They left their cities, abandoned the protection of the wall, and dispersed themselves in flight more desperately than before. The enemy, on the other hand, pursued them with more unrelenting cruelty than before, and butchered our countrymen like sheep, so that their habitations were like those of savage beasts; for they turned their arms upon each other, and for the sake of a little sustenance, imbrued their hands in the blood of their fellow countrymen. Thus foreign calamities were augmented by domestic feuds; so that the whole country was entirely destitute of provisions, save such as could be procured in the chase.

20. Again, therefore, the wretched remnant, sending to Aetius, a powerful Roman citizen, address him as follow: — 'To Aetius,* now consul for the third time: the groans of the Britons.' And again a little further, thus: — 'The barbarians drive us to the sea; the sea throws us back on the barbarians: thus two modes of death await us, we are either slain or drowned.' The Romans, however, could not assist them, and in the meantime the discomfited people, wandering in the woods, began to feel the effects of a severe famine, which compelled many of them without delay to yield themselves up to their cruel persecutors, to obtain subsistence: others of them, however, lying hid in mountains, caves and woods, continually sallied out from thence to renew the war. And then it was, for the first time, that they overthrew their enemies, who had for so many years been living in their country; for their trust was not in man, but in God; according to the maxim of Philo, 'We must have divine assistance, when that of man fails.' The boldness

---

* Or Agitius, according to another reading.

of the enemy was for a while checked, but not the wickedness of our countrymen; the enemy left our people, but the people did not leave their sins.

21. For it has always been a custom with our nation, as it is at present, to be impotent in repelling foreign foes, but bold and invincible in raising civil war, and bearing the burdens of their offences: they are impotent, I say, in following the standard of peace and truth, but bold in wickedness and falsehood. The audacious invaders therefore return to their winter quarters, determined before long again to return and plunder. And then, too, the Picts for the first time seated themselves at the extremity of the island, where they afterwards continued, occasionally plundering and wasting the country. During these truces, the wounds of the distressed people are healed, but another sore, still more venomous, broke out. No sooner were the ravages of the enemy checked, than the island was deluged with a most extraordinary plenty of all things, greater than was before known, and with it grew up every kind of luxury and licentiousness. It grew with so firm a root, that

one might truly say of it, 'Such fornication is heard of among you, as never was known the like among the Gentiles.' But besides this vice, there arose also every other, to which human nature is liable and in particular that hatred of truth, together with her supporters, which still at present destroys every thing good in the island; the love of falsehood, together with its inventors, the reception of crime in the place of virtue, the respect shown to wickedness rather than goodness, the love of darkness instead of the sun, the admission of Satan as an angel of light. Kings were anointed, not according to God's ordinance, but such as showed themselves more cruel than the rest; and soon after, they were put to death by those who had elected them, without any inquiry into their merits, but because others still more cruel were chosen to succeed them. If any one of these was of a milder nature than the rest, or in any way more regardful of the truth, he was looked upon as the ruiner of the country, every body cast a dart at him, and they valued things alike whether pleasing or displeasing to God, unless it so happened that what displeased him was pleasing to themselves. So that the words of the prophet, addressed to the people of old, might well be applied to our own countrymen: 'Children without a law, have ye left God and provoked to anger the holy one of Israel?* Why will ye still inquire, adding iniquity? Every head is languid and every heart is sad; from the sole of the foot to the crown, there is no health in him.' And thus they did all things contrary to their salvation, as if no remedy could be applied to the world by the true Physician of all men. And not only the laity did so, but our Lord's own flock and its shepherds, who ought to have been an example to the people, slumbered away their time in drunkenness, as if they had been dipped in wine; whilst the swellings of pride, the jar of strife, the griping talons of envy, and the confused estimate of right and wrong, got such entire possession of them, that there seemed to be poured out (and the same still continueth) contempt upon princes, and to be made by their vanities to wander astray and not in the way.

22. Meanwhile, God being willing to purify his family who were infected by so deep a stain of

---

* Isa. I. 4,5. In most of these quotations there is great verbal variation from the authorised version: the author probably quoted from memory, if not from the Latin version.

woe, and at the hearing only of their calamities to amend them; a vague rumour suddenly as if on wings reaches the ears of all, that their inveterate foes were rapidly approaching to destroy the whole country, and to take possession of it, as of old, from one end to the other. But yet they derived no advantage from this intelligence; for, like frantic beasts, taking the bit of reason between their teeth, they abandoned the safe and narrow road, and rushed forward upon the broad downward path of vice, which leads to death. Whilst, therefore, as Solomon says, the stubborn servant is not cured by words, the fool is scourged and feels it not: a pestilential disease morally affected the foolish people, which, without the sword, cut off so large a number of persons, that the living were not able to bury them. But even this was no warning to them, that in them also might be fulfilled the words of Isaiah the prophet, 'And God hath called his people to lamentation, to baldness, and to the girdle of sackcloth; behold they begin to kill calves, and to slay rams, to eat, to drink, and to say, "We will eat and drink, for to-morrow we shall die."' For the time was approaching, when all their iniquities, as formerly those of the

Amorrhaeans, should be fulfilled. For a council was called to settle what was best and most expedient to be done, in order to repel such frequent and fatal irruptions and plunderings of the above-named nations.

23. Then all the councillors, together with that proud tyrant Gurthrigern [Vortigern], the British king, were so blinded, that, as a protection to their country, they sealed its doom by inviting in among them like wolves into the sheep-fold), the fierce and impious Saxons, a race hateful both to God and men, to repel the invasions of the northern nations. Nothing was ever so pernicious to our country, nothing was ever so unlucky. What palpable darkness must have enveloped their minds — darkness desperate and cruel! Those very people whom, when absent, they dreaded more than death itself, were invited to reside, as one may say, under the selfsame roof. Foolish are the princes, as it is said, of Thafneos, giving counsel to unwise Pharaoh. A multitude of whelps came forth from the lair of this barbaric lioness, in three cyuls, as they call them, that is, in there ships of war, with their sails wafted by the wind and with omens and prophecies

favourable, for it was foretold by a certain soothsayer among them, that they should occupy the country to which they were sailing three hundred years, and half of that time, a hundred and fifty years, should plunder and despoil the same. They first landed on the eastern side of the island, by the invitation of the unlucky king, and there fixed their sharp talons, apparently to fight in favour of the island, but alas! more truly against it. Their mother-land, finding her first brood thus successful, sends forth a larger company of her wolfish offspring, which sailing over, join themselves to their bastard-born comrades. From that time the germ of iniquity and the root of contention planted their poison amongst us, as we deserved, and shot forth into leaves and branches. the barbarians being thus introduced as soldiers into the island, to encounter, as they falsely said, any dangers in defence of their hospitable entertainers, obtain an allowance of provisions, which, for some time being plentifully bestowed, stopped their doggish mouths. Yet they complain that their monthly supplies are not furnished in sufficient abundance, and they industriously aggravate each occasion of quarrel, saying that unless more liberality is shown them, they will break the treaty and plunder the whole island. In a short time, they follow up their threats with deeds.

24. For the fire of vengeance, justly kindled by former crimes, spread from sea to sea, fed by the hands of our foes in the east, and did not cease, until, destroying the neighbouring towns and lands, it reached the other side of the island, and dipped its red and savage tongue in the western ocean. In these assaults, therefore, not unlike that of the Assyrian upon Judea, was fulfilled in our case what the prophet describes in words of lamentation; 'They have burned with fire the sanctuary; they have polluted on earth the tabernacle of thy name.' And again, 'O God, the gentiles have come into thine inheritance; thy holy temple have they defiled,' &c. So that all the columns were levelled with the ground by the frequent strokes of the battering-ram, all the husbandmen routed, together with their bishops, priests, and people, whilst the sword gleamed, and the flames crackled around them on every side. Lamentable to behold, in the midst of the streets lay the tops of lofty towers, tumbled to the ground, stones of high walls, holy altars,

fragments of human bodies, covered with livid clots of coagulated blood, looking as if they had been squeezed together in a press; and with no chance of being buried, save in the ruins of the houses, or in the ravening bellies of wild beasts and birds; with reverence be it spoken for their blessed souls, if, indeed, there were many found who were carried, at that time, into the high heaven by the holy angels. So entirely had the vintage, once so fine, degenerated and become bitter, that, in the words of the prophet, there was hardly a grape or ear of corn to be seen where the husbandman had turned his back.

25. Some therefore, of the miserable remnant, being taken in the mountains, were murdered in great numbers; others, constrained by famine, came and yielded themselves to be slaves for ever to their foes, running the risk of being instantly slain, which truly was the greatest favour that could be offered them: some others passed beyond the seas with loud lamentations instead of the voice of exhortation. 'Thou hast given us as sheep to be slaughtered, and among the Gentiles hast thou dispersed us.' Others, committing the safeguard of their lives, which

were in continual jeopardy, to the mountains, precipices, thickly wooded forests, and to the rocks of the seas (albeit with trembling hearts), remained still in their country. But in the meanwhile, an opportunity happening, when these most cruel robbers were returned home, the poor remnants of our nation (to whom flocked from divers places round about our miserable countrymen as fast as bees to their hives, for fear of an ensuing storm), being strengthened by God, calling upon him with all their hearts, as the poet says, — 'With their unnumbered vows they burden heaven,' that they might not be brought to utter destruction, took arms under the conduct of Ambrosius Aurelianus, a modest man, who of all the Roman nation was then alone in the confusion of this troubled period by chance left alive. His parents, who for their merit were adorned with the purple, had been slain in these same broils, and now his progeny in these our days, although shamefully degenerated from the worthiness of their ancestors, provoke to battle their cruel conquerors, and by the goodness of our Lord obtain the victory.

26. After this, sometimes our countrymen, sometimes the enemy, won the field, to the end that our Lord might in this land try after his accustomed manner these his Israelites, whether they loved him or not, until the year of the siege of Bath-hill, when took place also the last almost, though not the least slaughter of our cruel foes, which was (as I am sure) forty-four years and one month after the landing of the Saxons, and also the time of my own nativity. And yet neither to this day are the cities of our country inhabited as before, but being forsaken and overthrown, still lie desolate; our foreign wars having ceased, but our civil troubles still remaining. For as well the remembrance of such terrible desolation of the island, as also of the unexpected recovery of the same, remained in the minds of those who were eyewitnesses of the wonderful events of both, and in regard thereof, kings, public magistrates, and private persons, with priests and clergymen, did all and every one of them live orderly according to their several vocations. But when these had departed out of this world, and a new race succeeded, who were ignorant of this troublesome time, and had only experience of the present prosperity, all the laws of truth and

justice were so shaken and subverted, that not so much as a vestige or remembrance of these virtues remained among the above-named orders of men, except among a very few who, compared with the great multitude which were daily rushing headlong down to hell, are accounted so small a number, that our reverend mother, the church, scarcely beholds them, her only true children, reposing in her bosom; whose worthy lives, being a pattern to al men, and beloved of God, inasmuch as by their holy prayers, as by certain pillars and most profitable supporters, our infirmity is sustained up, that it may not utterly be broken down, I would have no one suppose I intended to reprove, if forced by the increasing multitude of offences, I have freely, aye, with anguish, not so much declared as bewailed the wickedness of those who are become servants, not only to their bellies, but also to the devil rather than to Christ, who is our blessed God, world without end.

NENNIUS
THE HISTORY OF THE BRITONS

I. The Prologue

1. Nennius, the lowly minister and servant of the servants of God, by the grace of God, disciple of St. Elbotus,* to all the followers of truth sendeth health.

Be it known to your charity, that being dull in intellect and rude of speech, I have presumed to deliver these things in the Latin tongue, not trusting to my own learning, which is little or none at all, but partly from traditions of our ancestors, partly from writings and monuments of the ancient inhabitants of Britain, partly from the annals of the Romans, and the chronicles of the sacred fathers, Isidore, Hieronymus, Prosper, Eusebius, and from the histories of the Scots and Saxons, although our enemies, not following my

---

* Or Elvod, bishop of Bangor, A.D. 755, who first adopted in the Cambrian church the new cycle for regulating Easter.

own inclinations, but, to the best of my ability, obeying the commands of my seniors; I have lispingly put together this history from various sources, and have endeavoured, from shame, to deliver down to posterity the few remaining ears of corn about past transactions, that they might not be trodden under foot, seeing that an ample crop has been snatched away already by the hostile reapers of foreign nations. For many things have been in my way, and I, to this day, have hardly been able to understand, even superficially, as was necessary, the sayings of other men; much less was I able in my own strength, but like a barbarian, have I murdered and defiled the language of others. But I bore about with me an inward wound, and I was indignant, that the name of my own people, formerly famous and distinguished, should sink into oblivion, and like smoke be dissipated. But since, however, I had rather myself be the historian of the Britons than nobody, although so many are to be found who might much more satisfactorily discharge the labour thus imposed on me; I humbly entreat my readers, whose ears I may offend by the inelegance of my words, that they will fulfil the wish of my seniors, and grant me the easy task of listening with candour to my history. For zealous efforts very often fail: but bold enthusiasm, were it in its power, would not suffer me to fail. May, therefore, candour be shown where the inelegance of my words is insufficient, and may the truth of this history, which my rustic tongue has ventured, as a kind of plough, to trace out in furrows, lose none of its influence from that cause, in the ears of my hearers. For it is better to drink a wholesome draught of truth from the humble vessel, than poison mixed with honey from a golden goblet.

2. And do not be loath, diligent reader, to winnow my chaff, and lay up the wheat in the storehouse of your memory: for truth regards not who is the speaker, nor in what manner it is spoken, but that the thing be true; and she does not despise the jewel which she has rescued from the mud, but she adds it to her former treasures.

For I yield to those who are greater and more eloquent than myself, who, kindled with generous ardour, have endeavoured by Roman eloquence to smooth the jarring elements of their tongue, if they have left unshaken any pillar of history which I wished to see remain. This history therefore has been compiled from a wish to benefit my inferiors, not from envy of those who are superior to me, in the 858th year of our Lord's incarnation, and in the 24th year of Mervin, king of the Britons, and I hope that the prayers of my betters will be offered up for me in recompense of my labour. But this is sufficient by way of preface. I shall obediently accomplish the rest to the utmost of my power.

II. The Apology of Nennius

Here begins the apology of Nennius, the historiographer of the Britons, of the race of the Britons.

3. I, Nennius, disciple of St. Elbotus, have endeavoured to write some extracts which the dullness of the British nation had cast away, because teachers had no knowledge, nor gave any information in their books about this island of Britain. But I have got together all that I could find as well from the annals of the Romans as from the chronicles of the sacred fathers, Hieronymus, Eusebius, Isidorus, Prosper, and from the annals of the Scots and Saxons, and

from our ancient traditions. Many teachers and scribes have attempted to write this, but somehow or other have abandoned it from its difficulty, either on account of frequent deaths, or the often recurring calamities of war. I pray that every reader who shall read this book, may pardon me, for having attempted, like a chattering jay, or like some weak witness, to write these things, after they had failed. I yield to him who knows more of these things than I do.

III. The History

4, 5. From Adam to the flood, are two thousand and forty-two years. From the flood of Abraham, nine hundred and forty-two. From Abraham to Moses, six hundred.* From Moses to Solomon, and the first building of the temple, four hundred and forty-eight. From Solomon to the rebuilding of the temple, which was under Darius, king of the Persians, six hundred and twelve years are computed. From Darius to the ministry of our

---

* And forty, according to Stevenson's new edition. The rest of this chronology is much contracted in several of the manuscripts, and hardly two of them contain it exactly the same.

Lord Jesus Christ, and to the fifteenth year of the emperor Tiberius, are five hundred and forty-eight years. So that from Adam to the ministry of Christ and the fifteenth year of the emperor Tiberius, are five thousand two hundred and twenty-eight years. From the passion of Christ are completed nine hundred and forty-six; from his incarnation, nine hundred and seventy-six: being the fifth year of Edmund, king of the Angles.

6. The first age of the world is from Adam to Noah; the second from Noah to Abraham; the third from Abraham to David; the fourth from David to Daniel; the fifth to John the Baptist; the sixth from John to the judgment, when our Lord Jesus Christ will come to judge the living and the dead, and the world by fire.

The first Julius.
The second Claudius.
The third Severus.
The fourth Carinus.
The fifth Constantius.
The sixth Maximus.
The seventh Maximianus.

The eighth another Severus Aequantius.
The ninth Constantius.*

Here beginneth the history of the Britons, edited by Mark the anchorite, a holy bishop of that people.

7. The island of Britain derives its name from Brutus, a Roman consul. Taken from the south-west point it inclines a little towards the west, and to its northern extremity measures eight hundred miles, and is in breadth two hundred. It contains thirty three cities,† viz.

1. Cair ebrauc (York).
2. Cair ceint (Canterbury).
3. Cair gurcoc (Anglesey?).
4. Cair guorthegern‡
5. Cair custeint (Carnarvon).
6. Cair guoranegon (Worcester).
7. Cair segeint (Silchester).
8. Cair guin truis (Norwich, or Winwick).

---

* This list of the Roman emperors who visited Britain, is omitted in many of the MSS.

† V.R. Twenty-eight, twenty-one.

‡ Site unknown.

9. Cair merdin (Caermarthen).
10. Cair peris (Porchester).
11. Cair lion (Caerleon-upon-Usk).
12. Cair mencipit (Verulam).
13. Cair caratauc (Catterick).
14. Cair ceri (Cirencester).
15. Cair glout (Gloucester).
16. Cair luillid (Carlisle).
17. Cair grant (Grantchester, now Cambridge).
18. Cair daun (Doncaster), or Cair dauri (Dorchester).
19. Cair britoc (Bristol).
20. Cair meguaid (Meivod).
21. Cair mauiguid (Manchester).
22. Cair ligion (Chester).
23. Cair guent (Winchester, or Caerwent, in Monmouthshire).
24. Cair collon (Colchester, or St. Colon, Cornwall).
25. Cair londein (London).
26. Cair guorcon (Worren, or Woran, in Pembrokeshire).
27. Cair lerion (Leicester).
28. Cair draithou (Drayton).
29. Cair pensavelcoit (Pevensey, in Sussex).
30. Cairtelm (Teyn-Grace, in Devonshire).

31. Cair Urnahc (Wroxeter, in Shropshire).
32. Cair colemion (Camelet, in Somersetshire).
33. Cair loit coit (Lincoln).

These are the names of the ancient cities of the island of Britain. It has also a vast many promontories, and castles innumerable, built of brick and stone. Its inhabitants consist of four different people; the Scots, the Picts, the Saxons and the ancient Britons.

8. Three considerable islands belong to it; one, on the south, opposite the Armorican shore, called Wight;* another between Ireland and Britain, called Eubonia or Man; and another directly north, beyond the Picts, named Orkney; and hence it was anciently a proverbial expression, in reference to its kings and rulers, 'He reigned over Britain and its three islands.'

9. It is fertilized by several rivers, which traverse it in all directions, to the east and west, to the south and north; but there are two pre-eminently distinguished among the rest, the Thames and the Severn, which formerly, like the two arms of Britain, bore the ships employed in the

* Inis-gueith, or Gueith.

conveyance of riches acquired by commerce. The Britons were once very populous, and exercised extensive dominion from sea to sea.

10.* Respecting the period when this island became inhabited subsequently to the flood, I have seen two distinct relations. According to the annals of the Roman history, the Britons deduce their origin both from the Greeks and Romans. On the side of the mother, from Lavinia, the daughter of Latinus, king of Italy, and of the race of Silvanus, the son of Inachus, the son of Dardanus; who was the son of Saturn, king of the Greeks, and who, having possessed himself of a part of Asia, built the city of Troy. Dardanus was the father of Troius, who was the father of Priam and Anchises; Anchises was the father of Aeneas, who was the father of Ascanius and Silvius; and this Silvius was the son of Aeneas and Lavinia, the daughter of the king of Italy. From the sons of Aeneas and Lavinia descended Romulus and Remus, who were the sons of the holy queen Rhea, and the founders of Rome. Brutus was consul when he conquered Spain, and reduced

---

* The whole of this, as far as the end of the paragraph, is omitted in several MSS.

that country to a Roman province. He afterwards subdued the island of Britain, whose inhabitants were the descendants of the Romans, from Silvius Posthumus. He was called Posthumus because he was born after the death of Aeneas his father; and his mother Lavinia concealed herself during her pregnancy; he was called Silvius, because he was born in a wood. Hence the Roman kings were called Silvan, and the Britons from Brutus, and rose from the family of Brutus.

Aeneas, after the Trojan war, arrived with his son in Italy; and Having vanquished Turnus, married Lavinia, the daughter of king Latinus, who was the son of Faunus, the son of Picus, the son of Saturn. After the death of Latinus, Aeneas obtained the kingdom Of the Romans, and Lavinia brought forth a son, who was named Silvius. Ascanius founded Alba, and afterwards married. And Lavinia bore to Aeneas a son, named Silvius; but Ascanius* married a wife, who conceived and became pregnant. And Aeneas, having been informed that his daughter-in-law was pregnant, ordered his son to send his magician to examine his wife, whether the child

---

*   Other MSS. Silvius.

conceived were male or female. The magician came and examined the wife and pronounced it to be a son, who should become the most valiant among the Italians, and the most beloved of all men.* In consequence of this prediction, the magician was put to death by Ascanius; but it happened that the mother of the child dying at its birth, he was named Brutus; ad after a certain interval, agreeably to what the magician had foretold, whilst he was playing with some others he shot his father with an arrow, not intentionally but by accident.† He was, for this cause, expelled from Italy, and came to the islands of the Tyrrhene sea, when he was exiled on account of the death of Turnus, slain by Aeneas. He then went among the Gauls, and built the city of the Turones, called Turnis.‡ At length he came to this island named from him Britannia, dwelt there, and filled it with his own descendants, and it has been inhabited from that time to the present period.

* V.R. Who should slay his father and mother, and be hated by all mankind.
† V.R. He displayed such superiority among his playfellows, that they seemed to consider him as their chief.
‡ Tours.

11. Aeneas reigned over the Latins three years; Ascanius thirty three years; after whom Silvius reigned twelve years, and Posthumus thirty-nine * years: the latter, from whom the kings of Alba are called Silvan, was brother to Brutus, who governed Britain at the time Eli the high-priest judged Israel, and when the ark of the covenant was taken by a foreign people. But Posthumus his brother reigned among the Latins.

12. After an interval of not less than eight hundred years, came the Picts, and occupied the Orkney Islands: whence they laid waste many regions, and seized those on the left hand side of Britain, where they still remain, keeping possession of a third part of Britain to this day.†

13. Long after this, the Scots arrived in Ireland from Spain. The first that came was Partholomus,‡ with a thousand men and women; these increased to four thousand; but a mortality coming suddenly upon them, they all perished in

---

* V.R. Thirty-seven.

† See Bede's Eccles. Hist.

‡ V.R. Partholomaeus, or Bartholomaeus.

one week. The second was Nimech, the son of...,* who, according to report, after having been at sea a year and a half, and having his ships shattered, arrived at a port in Ireland, and continuing there several years, returned at length with his followers to Spain. After these came three sons of a Spanish soldier with thirty ships, each of which contained thirty wives; and having remained there during the space of a year, there appeared to them, in the middle of the sea, a tower of glass, the summit of which seemed covered with men, to whom they often spoke, but received no answer. At length they determined to besiege the tower; and after a year's preparation, advanced towards it, with the whole number of their ships, and all the women, one ship only excepted, which had been wrecked, and in which were thirty men, and as many women; but when all had disembarked on the shore which surrounded the tower, the sea opened and swallowed them up. Ireland, however, was peopled, to the present period, from the family remaining in the vessel which was wrecked. Afterwards, other came from Spain,

---

* A blank is here in the MS. Agnomen is found in some of the others.

and possessed themselves of various parts of Britain.

14. Last of all came one Hoctor,* who continued there, and whose descendants remain there to this day. Istoreth, the son of Istorinus, with his followers, held Dalrieta; Buile had the island Eubonia, and other adjacent places. The sons of Liethali† obtained the country of the dimetae, where is a city called Menavia,‡ and the province Guiher and Cetgueli,§ which they held till they were expelled from every part of Britain, by Cunedda and his sons.

15. According to the most learned among the Scots, if any one desires to learn what I am now going to state, Ireland was a desert, and uninhabited, when the children of Israel crossed the Red Sea, in which, as we read in the Book of the Law, the Egyptians who followed them were drowned. At that period, there lived among this

---

* V.R. Damhoctor, Clamhoctor, and Elamhoctor.

† V.R. Liethan, Bethan, Vethan.

‡ St. David's.

§ Guiher, probably the Welsh district Gower. Cetgueli is Caer Kidwelly, in Carmarthenshire.

people, with a numerous family, a Scythian of noble birth, who had been banished from his country and did not go to pursue the people of God. The Egyptians who were left, seeing the destruction of the great men of their nation, and fearing lest he should possess himself of their territory, took counsel together, and expelled him. Thus reduced, he wandered forty-two years in Africa, and arrived, with his family, at the altars of the Philistines, by the Lake of Osiers. Then passing between Rusicada and the hilly country of Syria, they travelled by the river Malva through Mauritania as far as the Pillars of Hercules; and crossing the Tyrrhene Sea, landed in Spain, where they continued many years, having greatly increased and multiplied. Thence, a thousand and two years after the Egyptians were lost in the Red Sea, they passed into Ireland, and the district of Dalrieta.* At that period, Brutus, who first exercised the consular office, reigned over the Romans; and the state, which before was governed by regal power, was afterwards ruled, during four hundred and forty-seven years, by consuls, tribunes of the people, and dictators.

* North-western part of Antrim in Ulster.

The Britons came to Britain in the third age of the world; and in the fourth, the Scots took possession of Ireland.

The Britons who, suspecting no hostilities, were unprovided with the means of defence, were unanimously and incessantly attacked, both by the Scots from the west, and by the Picts from the north. A long interval after this, the Romans obtained the empire of the world.

16. From the first arrival of the Saxons into Britain, to the fourth year of king Mermenus, are computed four hundred and twenty eight years; from the nativity of our Lord to the coming of St. Patrick among the Scots, four hundred and five years; from the death of St. Patrick to that of St. Bridget, forty years; and from the birth of Columeille* to the death of St Bridget four years.†

---

* V.R. Columba.

† Some MSS. add, the beginning of the calculation is 23 cycles of 19 years from the incarnation of our Lord to the arrival of St. Patrick in Ireland, and they make 438 years. And from the arrival of St. Patrick to the cycle of 19 years in which we live are 22 cycles, which make 421 years.

17. I have learned another account of this Brutus from the ancient books of our ancestors.* After the deluge, the three sons of Noah severally occupied three different parts of the earth: Shem extended his borders into Asia, Ham into Africa, and Japheth in Europe.

The first man that dwelt in Europe was Alanus, with his three sons, Hisicion, Armenon, and Neugio. Hisicion had four sons, Francus, Romanus, Alamanus, and Brutus. Armenon had five sons, Gothus, Valagothus, Cibidus, Burgundus, and Longobardus. Neugio had three sons, Vandalus, Saxo, and Boganus. From Hisicion arose four nations — the Franks, the Latins, the Germans, and Britons: from Armenon, the Gothi, Balagothi, Cibidi, Burgundi, and Longobardi: from Neugio, the Bogari, Vandali, Saxones, and Tarinegi. The whole of Europe was subdivided into these tribes.

Alanus is said to have been the son of Fethuir;† Fethuir, the son of Ogomuin, who was the son of Thoi; Thoi was the son of Boibus,

---

* This proves the tradition of Brutus to be older than Geoffrey or Tyssilio, unless these notices of Brutus have been interpolated in the original work of Nennius.

† This genealogy is different in almost all the MSS.

Boibus of Semion, Semion of Mair, Mair of Ecthactus, Ecthactus of Aurthack, Aurthack of Ethec, Ethec of Ooth, Ooth of Aber, Aber of Ra, Ra of Esraa, Esraa of Hisrau, Hisrau of Bath, Bath of Jobath, Jobath of Joham, Joham of Japheth, Japheth of Noah, Noah of Lamech, Lamech of Mathusalem, Mathusalem of Enoch, Enoch of Jared, Jared of Malalehel, Malalehel of Cainan, Cainan of Enos, Enos of Seth, Seth of Adam, and Adam was formed by the living God. We have obtained this information respecting the original inhabitants of Britain from ancient tradition.

18. The Britons were thus called from Brutus: Brutus was the son of Hisicion, Hisicion was the son of Alanus, Alanus was the son of Rhea Silvia, Fhea Silvia was the daughter of Numa Pompilius, Numa was the son of Ascanius, Ascanius of Eneas, Eneas of Anchises, Anchises of Troius, Troius of Dardanus, Dardanus of Flisa, Flisa of Juuin, Juuin of Japheth; but Japheth had seven sons; from the first named Gomer, descended the Galli; from the second, Magog, the Scythi and Gothi; from the third, Madian, the Medi; from the fourth, Juuan, the Greeks; from the fifth, Tubal, arose the Hebrei, Hispani, and Itali; from the sixth, Mosoch,

sprung the Cappadoces; and from the seventh, named Tiras, descended the Thraces: these are the sons of Japheth, the son of Noah, the son of Lamech.

19.* The Romans, having obtained the dominion of the world, sent legates or deputies to the Britons to demand of them hostages and tribute, which they received from all other countries and islands; but they, fierce, disdainful, and haughty, treated the legation with contempt.

Then Julius Caesar, the first who had acquired absolute power at Rome, highly incensed against the Britons, sailed with sixty vessels to the mouth of the Thames, where they suffered shipwreck whilst he fought against Dolobellus, (the proconsul of the British king, who was called Belinus, and who was the son of Minocannus who governed all the islands of the Tyrrhene Sea), and thus Julius Caesar returned home without victory, having had his soldiers Slain, and his ships shattered.

---

* Some MSS. add, I will now return to the point from which I made this digression.

20. But after three years he again appeared with a large army, and three hundred ships, at the mouth of the Thames, where he renewed hostilities. In this attempt many of his soldiers and horses were killed; for the same consul had placed iron pikes in the shallow part of the river, and this having been effected with so much skill and secrecy as to escape the notice of the Roman soldiers, did them considerable injury; thus Caesar was once more compelled to return without peace or victory. The Romans were, therefore, a third time sent against the Britons; and under the command of Julius, defeated them near a place called Trinovantum (London), forty-seven years before the birth of Christ, and five thousand two hundred and twelve years from the creation.

Julius was the first exercising supreme power over the Romans who invaded Britain: in honour of him the Romans decreed the fifth month to be called after his name. He was assassinated in the Curia, in the ides of March, and Octavius Augustus succeeded to the empire of the world. He was the only emperor who received tribute from the Britons, according to the following verse of Virgil: 'Purpurea intexti tollunt aulaea Britanni.'

21. The second after him, who came into Britain, was the emperor Claudius, who reigned forty-seven years after the birth of Christ. He carried with him war and devastation; and, though not without loss of men, he at length conquered Britain. He next sailed to the Orkneys, which he likewise conquered, and afterwards rendered tributary. No tribute was in his time received from the Britons; but it was paid to British emperors. He reigned thirteen years and eight months. His monument is to be seen at Moguntia (among the Lombards), where he died in his way to Rome.

22. After the birth of Christ, one hundred and sixty-seven years, king Lucius, with all the chiefs of the British people, received baptism, in consequence of a legation sent by the Roman emperors and pope Evaristus.*

---

* V.R. Eucharistus. A marginal note in the Arundel MS. adds, 'He is wrong, because the first year of Evaristus was A.D. 79, whereas the first year of Eleutherius, whom he ought to have named, was A.D. 161.' Usher says, that in one MS. of Nennius he found the name of Eleutherius.

23. Severus was the third emperor who passed the sea to Britain, where, to protect the provinces recovered from barbaric incursions, he ordered a wall and a rampart to be made between the Britons, the Scots, and the Picts, extending across the island from sea to sea, in length one hundred and thirty-three miles: and it is called in the British language Gwal.* Moreover, he ordered it to be made between the Britons, and the Picts and Scots; for the Scots from the west, and the Picts from the north, unanimously made war against the Britons; but were at peace among themselves. Not long after Severus dies in Britain.

24. The fourth was the emperor and tyrant, Carausius, who, incensed at the murder of

---

* Or, the Wall. One MS. here adds, 'The above-mentioned Severus constructed it of rude workmanship in length 132 miles; i.e. from Penguaul, which village is called in Scottish Cenail, in English Peneltun, to the mouth of the river Cluth and Cairpentaloch, where this wall terminates; but it was of no avail. The emperor Carausius afterwards rebuilt it, and fortified it with seven castles between the two mouths: he built also a round house of polished stones on the banks of the river Carun (Carron): he likewise erected a triumphal arch, on which he inscribed his own name in memory of his victory.'

Severus, passed into Britain, and attended by the leaders of the Roman people, severely avenged upon the chiefs and rulers of the Britons, the cause of Severus.*

25. The fifth was Constantius the father of Constantine the Great. He died in Britain; his sepulchre, as it appears by the inscription on his tomb, is still seen near the city named Cair segont (near Carnarvon). Upon the pavement of the above-mentioned city he sowed three seeds of gold, silver and brass, that no poor person might ever be found in it. It is also called Minmanton.†

26. Maximianus‡ was the sixth emperor that ruled in Britain. It was in his time that consuls§

---

* This passage is corrupt, the meaning is briefly given in the translation.
† V.R. Mirmantum, Mirmantun, Minmanto, Minimantone. The Segontium of Antoninus, situated on a small river named Seiont, near Caernarfon.
‡ This is an inaccuracy of Nennius; Maximus and Maximianus were one and the same person; or rather no such person as Maximianus ever reigned in Britain.
§ Geoffrey of Monmouth gives the title of consul to several British generals who lived after this time. It is not unlikely that the town, name, and dignity, still lingered

began, and that the appellation of Caesar was discontinued: at this period also, St. Martin became celebrated for his virtues and miracles, and held a conversation with him.

27. The seventh emperor was Maximus. He withdrew from Britain with all his military force, slew Gratian, the king of the Romans, and obtained the sovereignty of all Europe. Unwilling to send back his warlike companions to their wives, children, and possessions in Britain, he conferred upon them numerous districts from the lake on the summit of Mons Jovis, to the city called Cant Guic, and to the western Tumulus, that is, to Cruc Occident.* These are the Armoric Britons, and they remain there to the present day. In consequence of their absence, Britain being overcome by foreign nations, the lawful heirs were cast out, till God interposed with his assistance. We are informed by the tradition of our ancestors that seven emperors went into

in the provinces after the Romans were gone, particularly as the cities of Britain maintained for a time a species of independence.

* This district, in modern language, extended from the great St. Bernard in Piedmont to Cantavic in Picardy, and from Picardy to the western coast of France.

Britain, though the Romans affirm there were nine.

28. Thus, agreeably to the account given by the Britons, the Romans governed them four hundred and nine years.

After this, the Britons despised the authority of the Romans, equally refusing to pay them tribute, or to receive their kings; nor durst the Romans any longer attempt the government of a country, the natives of which massacred their deputies.

29. We must now return to the tyrant Maximus. Gratian, with his brother Valentinian, reigned seven years. Ambrose, bishop of Milan, was then eminent for his skill in the dogmata of the Catholics. Valentinianus and Theodosius reigned eight years. At that time a synod was held at Constantinople, attended by three hundred and fifty of the fathers, and in which all heresies were condemned. Jerome, the presbyter of Bethlehem, was then universally celebrated. Whilst Gratian exercised supreme dominion over the world, Maximus, in a sedition of the soldiers, was saluted emperor in Britain, and soon after crossed the sea to Gaul. At Paris, by the treachery

of Mellobaudes, his master of the horse, Gratian was defeated and fleeing to Lyons, was taken and put to death; Maximus afterwards associated his son victor in the government.

Martin, distinguished for his great virtues, was at this period bishop of Tours. After a considerable space of time, Maximus was divested of royal power by the consuls Valentinianus and Theodosius, and sentenced to be beheaded at the third mile-stone from Aquileia: in the same year also his son Victor was killed in Gaul by Arbogastes, five thousand six hundred and ninety years from the creation of the world.

30. Thrice were the Roman deputies put to death by the Britons, and yet these, when harassed by the incursions of the barbarous nations, viz. Of the Scots and Picts, earnestly solicited the aid of the Romans. To give effect to their entreaties, ambassadors were sent, who made their entrance with impressions of deep sorrow, having their heads covered with dust, and carrying rich presents, to expiate the murder of the deputies. They were favourably received by the consuls,

and swore submission to the Roman yoke, with whatever severity it might be imposed.

The Romans, therefore, came with a powerful army to the assistance of the Britons; and having appointed over them a ruler, and settled the government, returned to Rome: and this took place alternately during the space of three hundred and forty-eight years. The Britons, however, from the oppression of the empire, again massacred The Roman deputies, and again petitioned for succour. Once more the Romans undertook the government of the Britons, and assisted them in repelling their neighbours; and, after having exhausted the country of its gold, silver, brass, honey, and costly vestments, and having besides received rich gifts, they returned in great triumph to Rome.

31. After the above-said war between the Britons and Romans, the assassination of their rulers, and the victory of Maximus, who slew Gratian, and the termination of the Roman power in Britain, they were in alarm forty years.

Vortigern then reigned in Britain. In his time, the natives had cause of dread, not only from the inroads of the Scots and Picts, but also from the Romans, and their apprehensions of Ambrosius.*

In the meantime, three vessels, exiled from Germany, arrived in Britain. They were commanded by Horsa and Hengist, brothers, and sons of Wihtgils. Wihtgils was the son of Witta; Witta of Wecta; Wecta of Woden; Woden of Frithowald; Frithowald of Frithuwulf; Frithuwulf of Finn; Finn of Godwulf; Godwulf of Geat, who, as they say, was the son of a god, not† of the omnipotent God and our Lord Jesus Christ (who before the beginning of the world, was with the Father and the Holy Spirit, co-eternal and of the same substance, and who, in compassion to human nature, disdained not to assume the form of a servant), but the offspring of one of their idols, and whom, blinded by some demon, they worshipped according to the custom of the

---

* These words relate evidently to some cause of dispute between the Romans, Ambrosius, and Vortigern. Vortigern is said to have been sovereign of the Dimetae, and Ambrosius son to the king of the Damnonii. The latter was half a Roman by descent, and naturally supported the Roman interest: the former was entirely a Briton, and as naturally seconded by the original Britons.

† V.R. not the God of gods, the Amen, the Lord of Hosts, but one of their idols which they worshipped.

heathen. Vortigern received them as friends, and delivered up to them the island which is in their language called Thanet, and, by the Britons, Ruym.* Gratianus Aequantius at that time reigned in Rome. The Saxons were received by Vortigern, four hundred and forty-seven years after the passion of Christ, and,† according to the tradition of our ancestors, from the period of their first arrival in Britain, to the first year of the reign of king Edmund, five hundred and forty-two years; and to that in which we now write, which is the fifth of his reign, five hundred and forty-seven years.

32. At that time St. Germanus, distinguished for his numerous virtues, came to preach in Britain: by his ministry many were saved; but many likewise died unconverted. Of the various miracles which God enabled him to perform, I shall here mention only a few: I shall first advert

---

* Sometimes called Ruoichin, Ruith-in, or 'river island,' separated from the rest of Kent and the mainland of Britain by the estuary of the Wantsum, which, though now a small brook, was formerly navigable for large vessels, and in Bede's time was three stadia broad, and fordable only at two places.

† The rest of this sentence is omitted in some of the MSS.

to that concerning an iniquitous and tyrannical king, named Benlli.* The holy man, informed of his wicked conduct, hastened to visit him, for the purpose of remonstrating him. When the man of God, with his attendants, arrived at the gate of the city, they were respectfully received by the keeper of it, who came out and saluted them. Him they commissioned to communicate their intention to the king, who returned a harsh answer, declaring, with an oath, that although they remained there a year, they should not enter the city. While waiting for an answer, the evening came on, and they knew not where to go. At length, came one of the king's servants, who bowing himself before the man of God, announced the words of the tyrant, inviting them, at the same time, to his own house, to which they went, and were kindly received. It happened, however, that he had no cattle, except one cow and a calf, the latter of which, urged by generous hospitality to his guests, he killed, dressed and set before them. But holy St. Germanus ordered his companions not to break a

---

* King of Powys. V.R. Benli in the district of Iâl (in Derbyshire); in the district of Dalrieta; Belinus; Beluni; and Benty.

bone of the calf; and, the next morning, it was found alive uninjured, and standing by its mother.

33. Early the same day, they again went to the gate of the city, to solicit audience of the wicked king; and, whilst engaged in fervent prayer they were waiting for admission, a man, covered with sweat, came out, and prostrated himself before them. Then St. Germanus, addressing him, said 'Dost thou believe in the Holy Trinity?' To which the man having replied, 'I do believe,' he baptized, and kissed him, saying, 'Go in peace; within this hour thou shalt die: the angels of God are waiting for thee in the air; with them thou shalt ascent to that God in whom thou has believed.' He, overjoyed, entered the city, and being met by the prefect, was seized, bound, and conducted before the tyrant, who having passed sentence upon him, he was immediately put to death; for it was a law of this wicked king, that whoever was not at his labour before sun-rising should be beheaded in the citadel. In the meantime, St. Germanus, with his attendants, waited the whole day before the gate, without obtaining admission to the tyrant.

34. The man above-mentioned, however, remained with them. 'Take care,' said St. Germanus to him, 'that none of your friends remain this night within these walls.' Upon this he hastily entered the city, brought out his nine sons, and with them retired to the house where he had exercised such generous hospitality. Here St. Germanus ordered them to continue, fasting; and when the gates were shut, 'Watch,' said he, 'and whatever shall happen in the citadel, turn not thither your eyes; but pray without ceasing, and invoke the protection of the true God.' And, behold, early in the night, fire fell from heaven, and burned the city, together with all those who were with the tyrant, so that not one escaped; and that citadel has never been rebuilt even to this day.

35. The following day, the hospitable man who had been converted by the preaching of St. Germanus, was baptized, with his sons, and all the inhabitants of that part of the country; and St. Germanus blessed him, saying, 'a king shall not be wanting of thy seed for ever.' The name of

this person is Catel Drunlue:* 'from henceforward thou shalt be a king all the days of thy life.' Thus was fulfilled the prophecy of the Psalmist: 'He raiseth up the poor out of the dust, and lifteth up the needy out of the dunghill.' And agreeably to the prediction of St. Germanus, from a servant he became a king: all his sons were kings, and from their offspring the whole country of Powys has been governed to this day.

36. After the Saxons had continued some time in the island of Thanet, Vortigern promised to supply them with clothing and provision, on condition they would engage to fight against the enemies of his country. But the barbarians having greatly increased in number, the Britons became incapable of fulfilling their engagement; and when the Saxons, according to the promise they had received, claimed a supply of provisions and clothing, the Britons replied, 'Your number is increased; your assistance is now unnecessary; you may, therefore, return home, for we can no longer support you;' and hereupon they began to

---

* Or Cadell Deyrnllug, prince of the Vale Royal and the upper part of Powys.

devise means of breaking the peace between them.

37. But Hengist, in whom united craft and penetration, perceiving he had to act with an ignorant king, and a fluctuating people, incapable of opposing much resistance, replied to Vortigern, 'We are, indeed, few in number; but, if you will give us leave, we will send to our country for an additional number of forces, with whom we will fight for you and your subjects.' Vortigern assenting to this proposal, messengers were despatched to Scythia, where selecting a number of warlike troops, they returned with sixteen vessels, bringing with them the beautiful daughter of Hengist. And now the Saxon chief prepared an entertainment, to which he invited the king, his officers, and Ceretic, his interpreter, having previously enjoined his daughter to serve them so profusely with wine and ale, that they might soon become intoxicated. This plan succeeded; and Vortigern, at the instigation of the devil, and enamoured with the beauty of the damsel, demanded her, through the medium of his interpreter, of the father, promising to give for her whatever he should ask. Then Hengist,

who had already consulted with the elders who attended him of the Oghgul* race, demanded for his daughter the province, called in English, Centland, in British, Ceint, (Kent.) This cession was made without the knowledge of the king, Guoyrancgonus,† who then reigned in Kent, and who experienced no inconsiderable share of grief, from seeing his kingdom thus clandestinely, fraudulently, and imprudently resigned to foreigners. Thus the maid was delivered up to the king, who slept with her, and loved her exceedingly.

38. Hengist, after this, said to Vortigern, 'I will be to you both a father and an adviser; despise not my counsels, and you shall have no reason to fear being conquered by any man or any nation whatever; for the people of my country are strong, warlike, and robust: if you approve, I will

---

* V.R. Who had come with him from the island of Oghgul, Oehgul (or Tingle), Angul. According to Gunn, a small island in the duchy of Sleswick in Denmark, now called Angel, of which Flensburg is the metropolis. Hence the origin of the Angles.

† V.R. Gnoiram cono, Goiranegono, Guiracgono. Malmesbury, Gorongi; Camden, Guorong, supposed to mean governor, or viceroy.

send for my son and his brother, both valiant men, who at my invitation will fight against the Scots, and you can give them the countries in the north, near the wall called Gual.'* The incautious sovereign having assented to this, Octa and Ebusa arrived with forty ships. In these they sailed round the country of the Picts, laid waste the Orkneys, and took possession of many regions, even to the Pictish confines.†

But Hengist continued, by degrees, sending for ships from his own country, so that some islands whence they came were left without inhabitants; and whilst his people were increasing in power and number, they came to the above-named province of Kent.

39. In the meantime, Vortigern, as if desirous of adding to the evils he had already occasioned, married his own daughter, by whom he had a son. When this was made known to St. Germanus, he came, with all the British clergy, to reprove him: and whilst a numerous assembly of the

---

* Antoninus's wall.

† Some MSS. add, 'beyond the Frenesic, Fresicum (or Fresic) sea,' i.e. which is between us and the Scotch. The sea between Scotland and Ireland. Camden translates it 'beyond the Frith;' Langhorne says, 'Solway Frith.'

ecclesiastics and laity were in consultation, the weak king ordered his daughter to appear before them, and in the presence of all to present her son to St. Germanus, and declare that he was the father of the child. The immodest* woman obeyed; and St. Germanus, taking the child, said, 'I will be a father to you, my son; nor will I dismiss you till a razor, scissors, and comb, are given to me, and it is allowed you to give them to your carnal father.' The child obeyed St. Germanus, and going to his father Vortigern, said to him, 'Thou art my father; shave and cut the hair of my head.' The king blushed, and was silent; and, without replying to the child, arose in great anger, and fled from the presence of St. Germanus, execrated and condemned by the whole synod.

40. But soon after, calling together his twelve wise men, to consult what was to be done, they said to him, 'Retire to the remote boundaries of your kingdom; there build and fortify a city† to defend yourself, for the people you have received

---

* V.R. 'Immodest' is omitted in some MSS.

† V.R. You shall find a fortified city in which you may defend yourself.

are treacherous; they are seeking to subdue you by stratagem, and, even during your life, to seize upon all the countries subject to your power, how much more will they attempt, after your death!' The king, pleased with this advice, departed with his wise men, and travelled through many parts of his territories, in search of a place convenient for the purpose of building a citadel. Having, to no purpose, travelled far and wide, they came at length to a province called Guenet;* and having surveyed the mountains of Heremus,† they discovered, on the summit of one of them, a situation, adapted to the construction of a citadel. Upon this, the wise men said to the king, 'Build here a city: for, in this place, it will ever be secure against the barbarians.' Then the king sent for artificers, carpenters, stone-masons, and collected all the materials requisite to building; but the whole of these disappeared in one night, so that nothing remained of what had been provided for the constructing of the citadel.

---

* V.R. Guined, Guoienet, Guenez, North Wales.

† V.R. Heremi, Heriri, or Eryri, signifying eagle rocks, the mountains of Snowdon, in Caernarfonshire. The spot alluded to is supposed to be Dinas Emrys, or the fortress of Ambrosius.

Materials were, therefore, from all parts, procured a second and third time, and again vanished as before, leaving and rendering every effort ineffectual. Vortigern inquired of his wise men the cause of this opposition to his undertaking, and of so much useless expense of labour? They replied, 'You must find a child born without a father, put him to death, and sprinkle with his blood the ground on which the citadel is to be built, or you will never accomplish your purpose.'

41. In consequence of this reply, the king sent messengers throughout Britain, in search of a child born without a father. After having inquired in all the provinces, they came to the field of Aelecti,* in the district of Glevesing,† where a party of boys were playing at ball. And two of them quarrelling, one said to the other, 'O boy without a father, no good will ever happen to you.' Upon this, the messengers diligently inquired of the mother and the other boys,

---

* V.R. Elleti, Electi, Gleti. Supposed to be Bassalig in Monmouthshire.

† The district between the Usk and Rumney, in Monmouthshire.

whether he had had a father? Which his mother denied, saying, 'In what manner he was conceived I know not, for I have never had intercourse with any man;' and then she solemnly affirmed that he had no mortal father. The boy was, therefore, led away, and conducted before Vortigern the king.

42. A meeting took place the next day for the purpose of putting him to death. Then the boy said to the king, 'Why have your servants brought me hither?' 'That you may be put to death,' replied the king, 'and that the ground on which my citadel is to stand, may be sprinkled with your blood, without which I shall be unable to build it.' 'Who,' said the boy, 'instructed you to do this?' 'My wise men,' answered the king. 'Order them hither,' returned the boy; this being complied with, he thus questioned them: 'By what means was it revealed to you that this citadel could not be built, unless the spot were previously sprinkled with my blood? Speak without disguise, and declare who discovered me to you;' then turning to the king, 'I will soon,' said he, 'unfold to you every thing; but I desire to question your wise men, and wish them to

disclose to you what is hidden under this pavement:' they acknowledging their ignorance, 'there is,' said he, 'a pool; come and dig:' they did so, and found the pool. 'Now,' continued he, 'tell me what is in it;' but they were ashamed, and made no reply. 'I,' said the boy, 'can discover it to you: there are two vases in the pool;' they examined and found it so: continuing his questions, 'What is in the vases?' they were silent: 'there is a tent in them,' said the boy; 'separate them, and you shall find it so;' this being done by the king's command, there was found in them a folded tent. The boy, going on with his questions, asked the wise men what was in it? But they not knowing what to reply, 'There are,' said he, 'two serpents, one white and the other red; unfold the tent;' they obeyed, and two sleeping serpents were discovered; 'consider attentively,' said the boy, 'what they are doing.' The serpents began to struggle with each other; and the white one, raising himself up, threw down the other into the middle of the tent, and sometimes drove him to the edge of it; and this was repeated thrice. At length the red one, apparently the weaker of the two, recovering his strength, expelled the white one from the tent;

and the latter being pursued through the pool by the red one, disappeared. Then the boy, asking the wise men what was signified by this wonderful omen, and they expressing their ignorance, he said to the king, 'I will now unfold to you the meaning of this mystery. The pool is the emblem of this world, and the tent that of your kingdom: the two serpents are two dragons; the red serpent is your dragon, but the white serpent is the dragon of the people who occupy several provinces and districts of Britain, even almost from sea to sea: at length, however, our people shall rise and drive away the Saxon race from beyond the sea, whence they originally came; but do you depart from this place, where you are not permitted to erect a citadel; I, to whom fate has allotted this mansion, shall remain here; whilst to you it is incumbent to seek other provinces, where you may build a fortress.' 'What is your name?' asked the king; 'I am called Ambrose (in British Embresguletic),' returned the boy; and in answer to the king's question, 'What is your origin?' he replied, 'A Roman consul was my father.'

Then the king assigned him that city, with all the western Provinces of Britain; and departing with his wise men to the sinistral district, he arrived in the region named Gueneri, where he built a city which, according to his name, was called Cair Guorthegirn.*

43. At length Vortimer, the son of Vortigern, valiantly fought against Hengist, Horsa, and his people; drove them to the isle of Thanet, and thrice enclosed them within it, and beset them on the Western side.

The Saxons now despatched deputies to Germany to solicit large reinforcements, and an additional number of ships: having obtained these, they fought against the kings and princes of Britain, and sometimes extended their

---

* An ancient scholiast adds, 'He then built Guasmoric, near Lugubalia (Carlisle), a city which in English is called Palmecaster.' Some difference of opinion exists among antiquaries respecting the site of Vortigern's castle or city. Usher places it at Gwent, Monmouthshire, which name, he says, was taken from Caer-Went, near Chepstow. This appears to agree with Geoffrey's account, {illegible} See Usher's Britain. Eccles. cap. v. p.23. According to others, supposed to be the city from the ruins of which arose the castle of Gurthrenion, in Radnorshire, Camden's Britannia, p.479. Whitaker, however, says that Cair Guorthegirn was the Maridunum of the Romans, and the present Caermarthen. (Hist. Of Manchester, book ii. c. 1.) See also Nennius, sec.47.

boundaries by victory, and sometimes were conquered and driven back.

44. Four times did Vortimer valorously encounter the enemy;* the first has been mentioned, the second was upon the river Darent, the third at the Ford, in their language called Epsford, though in ours Set thirgabail,† there Horsa fell, and Catigern, the son of Vortigern; the fourth battle he fought was near the stone‡ on the shore of the

---

* Some MSS. here add, 'This Vortimer, the son of Vortigern, in a synod held at Guartherniaun, after the wicked king, on account of the incest committed with his daughter, fled from the face of Germanus and the British clergy, would not consent to his father's wickedness; but returning to St. Germanus, and falling down at his feet, he sued for pardon; and in atonement for the calumny brought upon Germanus by his father and sister, gave him the land, in which the fore-mentioned bishop had endured such abuse, to be his for ever. Whence, in memory of St. Germanus, it received the name Guarenniaun (Guartherniaun, Gurthrenion, Gwarth Ennian) which signifies, a calumny justly retorted, since, when he thought to reproach the bishop, he covered himself with reproach.'

† According to Langhorne, Epsford was afterwards called, in the British tongue, Saessenaeg habail, or 'the slaughter of the Saxons.'

Gallic sea, where the Saxons being defeated, fled to their ships.

After a short interval Vortimer died; before his decease, anxious for the future prosperity of his country, he charged his friends to inter his body at the entrance of the Saxon port, viz. upon the rock where the Saxons first landed; 'for though,' said he, 'they may inhabit other parts of Britain, yet if you follow my commands, they will never remain in this island.' They imprudently disobeyed this last injunction, and neglected to bury him where he had appointed.*

45. After this the barbarians became firmly incorporated, and were assisted by foreign pagans; for Vortigern was their friend, on account of the daughter† of Hengist, whom he so much loved, that no one durst fight against him — in the meantime they soothed the imprudent king, and whilst practising every appearance of fondness, were plotting with his enemies. And let

‡ V.R. 'The Stone of Titulus,' thought to be Stone in Kent, or Larger-stone in Suffolk.

* Rapin says he was buried at Lincoln; Geoffrey, at London.

† V.R. Of his wife, and no one was able manfully to drive them off because they had occupied Britain not from their own valour, but by God's permission.

him that reads understand, that the Saxons were victorious, and ruled Britain, not from their superior prowess, but on account of the great sins of the Britons: God so permitting it.

For what wise man will resist the wholesome counsel of God? The Almighty is the King of kings, and the Lord of lords, ruling and judging every one, according to his own pleasure.

After the death of Vortimer, Hengist being strengthened by new accessions, collected his ships, and calling his leaders together, consulted by what stratagem they might overcome Vortigern and his army; with insidious intention they sent messengers to the king, with offers of peace and perpetual friendship; unsuspicious of treachery, the monarch, after advising with his elders, accepted the proposals.

46. Hengist, under pretence of ratifying the treaty, prepared an entertainment, to which he invited the king, the nobles, and military officers, in number about three hundred; speciously concealing his wicked intention, he ordered three hundred Saxons to conceal each a knife under his feet, and to mix with the Britons; 'and when,' said he, 'they are sufficiently inebriated,

&c. cry out, "Nimed eure Saxes," then let each draw his knife, and kill his man; but spare the king, on account of his marriage with my daughter, for it is better that he should be ransomed than killed.'*

The king with his company, appeared at the feast; and mixing with the Saxons, who, whilst they spoke peace with their tongues, cherished treachery in their hearts, each man was placed next to his enemy.

After they had eaten and drunk, and were much intoxicated, Hengist suddenly vociferated, 'Nimed eure Saxes!' and instantly his adherents drew their knives, and rushing upon the Britons, each slew him that sat next to him, and there was slain three hundred of the nobles of Vortigern. The king being a captive, purchased his redemption, by delivering up the three provinces of East, South, and Middle Sex, besides other districts at the option of his betrayers.

47. St. Germanus admonished Vortigern to turn to the true God, and abstain from all unlawful intercourse with his daughter; but the unhappy

---

* The VV. RR. of this section are too numerous to be inserted.

wretch fled for refuge to the province Guorthegirnaim,* so called from his own name, where he concealed himself with his wives: but St. Germanus followed him with all the British clergy, and upon a rock prayed for his sins during forty days and forty nights.

The Blessed man was unanimously chosen commander against the Saxons. And then, not by the clang of trumpets, but by praying, singing hallelujah, and by the cries of the army to God, the enemies were routed, and driven even to the sea.†

Again Vortigern ignominiously flew from St. Germanus to the kingdom of the Dimetae, where, on the river Towy,‡ he built a castle, which he named Cair Guothergirn. The saint, as usual, followed him there, and with his clergy fasted and prayed to the Lord three days, and as many nights. On the third night, at the third hour, fire fell suddenly from heaven, and totally burned the castle. Vortigern, the daughter of Hengist, his other wives, and all the inhabitants, both men

---

* A district of Radnorshire, forming the present hundred of Rhaiadr.

† V.R. This paragraph is omitted in the MSS.

‡ The Tobias of Ptolemy

and women, miserably perished: such was the end of this unhappy king, as we find written in the life of St. Germanus.

48. Others assure us, that being hated by all the people of Britain, for having received the Saxons, and being publicly charged by St. Germanus and the clergy in the sight of God, he betook himself to flight; and, that deserted and a wanderer, he sought a place of refuge, till broken hearted, he made an ignominious end.

Some accounts state, that the earth opened and swallowed him up, on the night his castle was burned; as no remains were discovered the following morning, either of him, or of those who were burned with him.

He had three sons: the eldest was Vortimer, who, as we have seen, fought four times against the Saxons, and put them to flight; the second Categirn, who was slain in the same battle with Horsa; the third was Pascent, who reigned in the two provinces Builth and Guorthegirnaim,* after the death of his father. These were granted him by Ambrosius, who was the great king among the

---

* In the northern part of the present counties of Radnor and Brecknock.

kings of Britain. The fourth was Faustus, born of an incestuous marriage with his daughter, who was brought up and educated by St. Germanus. He built a large monastery on the banks of the river Renis, called after his name, and which remains to the present period.*

49. This is the genealogy of Vortigern, which goes back to Fernvail,† who reigned in the kingdom of Guorthegirnai,‡ and was the son of Teudor; Teudor was the son of Pascent; Pascent of Guoidcant; Guoidcant of Moriud; Moriud of Eltat; Eltat of Eldoc; Eldoc of Paul; Paul of Meuprit; Meuprit of Braciat; Braciat of Pascent; Pascent of Guorthegirn, Guorthegirn of Guortheneu; Guortheneu of Guitaul; Guitaul of Guitolion; Guitolion of Gloui. Bonus, Paul, Mauron, Guotelin, were four brothers, who built Gloiuda, a great city upon the banks of the river Severn, and in Birtish is called Cair Gloui, in Saxon, Gloucester. Enough has been said of Vortigern.

---

* V.R. The MSS. add, 'and he had one daughter, who was the mother of St. Faustus.'

† Fernvail, or Farinmail, appears to have been king of Gwent or Monmouth.

‡ V.R. 'Two provinces, Builth and Guorthegirnaim.'

50. St. Germanus, after his death, returned into his own country.* At that time, the Saxons greatly increased in Britain, both in strength and numbers. And Octa, after the death of his father Hengist, came from the sinistral part of the island to the kingdom of Kent, and from him have proceeded all the kings of that province, to the present period.

Then it was, that the magnanimous Arthur, with all the kings and military force of Britain, fought against the Saxons. And though there were many more noble than himself, yet he was twelve times chosen their commander, and was as often conqueror. The first battle in which he was engaged, was at the mouth of the river Gleni.† The second, third, fourth, and fifth, were on another river, by the Britons called Duglas,‡ in the region Linuis. The sixth, on the river Bassas.§ The seventh in the wood Celidon, which the

* V.R. All this to the word 'Amen,' in other MSS. is placed after the legend of St. Patrick.

† Supposed by some to be the Glem, in Lincolnshire; but most probably the Glen, in the northern part of Northumberland.

‡ Or Dubglas. The little river Dunglas, which formed the southern boundary of Lothian. Whitaker says, the river Duglas, in Lancashire, near Wigan.

Britons call Cat Coit Celidon.* The eighth was near Gurnion castle,† where Arthur bore the image of the Holy Virgin,‡ mother of God, upon his shoulders, and through the power of our Lord Jesus Christ, and the holy Mary, put the Saxons to flight, and pursued them the whole day with great slaughter.§ The ninth was at the City of

§ Not a river, but an isolated rock in the Frith of Forth, near the town of North Berwick, called 'The Bass.' Some think it is the river Lusas, in Hampshire.

* The Caledonian forest; or the forest of Englewood, extending from Penrith to Carlisle.

† Variously supposed to be in Cornwall, or Binchester in Durham, but most probably the Roman station of Garionenum, near Yarmouth, in Norfolk.

‡ V.R. The image of the cross of Christ, and of the perpetual virgin St. Mary.

§ V.R. For Arthur proceeded to Jerusalem, and there made a cross to the size of the Saviour's cross, and there it was consecrated, and for three successive days he fasted, watched, and prayed, before the Lord's cross, that the Lord would give him the victory, by this sign, over the heathen; which also took place, and he took with him the image of St. Mary, the fragments of which are still preserved in great veneration at Wedale, in English Wodale, in Latin Vallis-doloris. Wodale is a village in the province of Lodonesia, but now of the jurisdiction of the bishop of St. Andrew's, of Scotland, six miles on the west of that heretofore noble and eminent monastery of

Legion,* which is called Cair Lion. The tenth was on the banks of the river Trat Treuroit.† The eleventh was on the mountain Breguoin, which we call Cat Bregion.‡ The twelfth was a most severe contest, when Arthur penetrated to the hill of Badon.§ In this engagement, nine hundred and forty fell by his hand alone, no one but the Lord affording him assistance. In all these engagements the Britons were successful. For no strength can avail against the will of the Almighty.

The more the Saxons were vanquished, the more they sought for new supplies of Saxons from Germany; so that kings, commanders, and military bands were invited over from almost every province. And this practice they continued till the reign of Ida, who was the son of Eoppa, he, of the Saxon race, was the first king in Bernicia, and in Cair Ebrauc (York).

   Meilros.
* Exeter.
† Or Ribroit, the Brue, in Somersetshire; or the Ribble, in Lancashire.
‡ Or Agned Cathregonion, Cadbury, in Somersetshire; or Edinburgh.
§ Bath.

When Gratian Aequantius was consul at Rome, because then the whole world was governed by the Roman consuls, the Saxons were received by Vortigern in the year of our Lord four hundred and forty-seven, and to the year in which we now write, five hundred and forty-seven. And whosoever shall read herein may receive instruction, the Lord Jesus Christ affording assistance, who, co-eternal with the Father and the Holy Ghost, lives and reigns for ever and ever. Amen.

In those days Saint Patrick was captive among the Scots. His master's name was Milcho, to whom he was a swineherd for seven years. When he had attained the age of seventeen he gave him his liberty. By the divine impulse, he applied himself to reading of the Scriptures, and afterwards went to Rome; where, replenished with the Holy Spirit, he continued a great while, studying the sacred mysteries of those writings. During his continuance there, Palladius, the first bishop, was sent by pope Celestine to convert the Scots (the Irish). But tempests and signs from God prevented his landing, for no one can arrive in any country, except it be allowed from above;

altering therefore his course from Ireland, he came to Britain and died in the land of the Picts.*

51. The death of Palladius being known, the Roman patricians, Theodosius and Valentinian, then reigning, pope Celestine sent Patrick to convert the Scots to the faith of the Holy Trinity; Victor, the angel of God, accompanying, admonishing, and assisting him, and also the bishop Germanus.

Germanus then sent the ancient Segerus with him as a venerable and praiseworthy bishop, to king Amatheus,† who lived near, and who had prescience of what was to happen; he was consecrated bishop in the reign of that king by the holy pontiff,‡ assuming the name of Patrick, having hitherto been known by that of Maun; Auxilius, Isserninus, and other brothers were ordained with him to inferior degrees.

---

* At Fordun, in the district of Mearns, in Scotland-Usher.

† V.R. Germanus 'sent the elder Segerus with him to a wonderful man, the holy bishop Amathearex.' Another MS. 'Sent the elder Segerus, a bishop, with him to Amatheorex.'

‡ V.R. 'Received the episcopal degree from the holy bishop Amatheorex.' Another MS. 'Received the episcopal degree from Matheorex and the holy bishop.'

52. Having distributed benedictions, and perfected all in the name of the Holy Trinity, he embarked on the sea which is between the Gauls and the Britons; and after a quick passage arrived in Britain, where he preached for some time. Every necessary preparation being made, and the angel giving him warning, he came to the Irish Sea. And having filled the ship with foreign gifts and spiritual treasures, by the permission of God he arrived in Ireland, where he baptized and preached.

53. From the beginning of the world, to the fifth year of king Logiore, when the Irish were baptized, and faith in the unity of the individual Trinity was published to them, are five thousand three hundred and thirty years.

54. Saint Patrick taught the gospel in foreign nations for the space of forty years. Endued with apostolical powers, he gave sight to the blind, cleansed the lepers, gave hearing to the deaf, cast out devils, raised nine from the dead, redeemed many captives of both sexes at his own charge, and set them free in the name of the Holy Trinity. He taught the servants of God, and he wrote three hundred and sixty-five canonical and other

books relating to the catholic faith. He founded as many churches, and consecrated the same number of bishops, strengthening them with the Holy Ghost. He ordained three thousand presbyters; and converted and baptized twelve thousand persons in the province of Connaught. And, in one day baptized seven kings, who were the seven sons of Amalgaid.* He continued fasting forty days and nights, on the summit of the mountain Eli, that is Cruachan-Aichle;† and preferred three petitions to God for the Irish, that had embraced the faith. The Scots say, the first was, that he would receive every repenting sinner, even at the latest extremity of life; the second, that they should never be exterminated by barbarians; and the third, that as Ireland‡ will be overflowed with water, seven years before the coming of our Lord to judge the quick and the dead, the crimes of the people might be washed away through his intercession, and their souls

---

* King of Connaught.

† A mountain in the west of Connaught, county of Mayo, now called Croagh-Patrick.

‡ V.R. that no Irishman may be alive on the day of judgment, because they will be destroyed seven years before in honour of St. Patrick.

purified at the last day. He gave the people his benediction from the upper part of the mountain, and going up higher, that he might pray for them; and that if it pleased God, he might see the effects of his labours, there appeared to him an innumerable flock of birds of many colours, signifying the number of holy persons of both sexes of the Irish nation, who should come to him as their apostle at the day of judgment, to be presented before the tribunal of Christ. After a life spent in the active exertion of good to mankind, St. Patrick, in a healthy old age, passed from this world to the Lord, and changing this life for a better, with the saints and elect of God he rejoices for evermore.

55. Saint Patrick resembled Moses in four particulars. The angel spoke to him in the burning bush. He fasted forty days and forty nights upon the mountain. He attained the period of one hundred and twenty years. No one knows his sepulchre, nor where he was buried; sixteen* years he was in captivity. In his twenty-fifth year, he was consecrated bishop by Saint

---

*   V.R. Fifteen.

Matheus,* and he was eighty-five years the apostle of the Irish. It might be profitable to treat more at large of the life of this saint, but it is now time to conclude this epitome of his labours.†

Here endeth the life of the holy bishop, Saint Patrick. After this, the MSS. give as 56, the legend of king Arthur, which in this edition occurs in 50.

The Genealogy of the Kings of Bernicia.‡

57. Woden begat Beldeg, who begat Beornec, who begat Gethbrond, who begat Aluson, who begat Ingwi, who begat Edibrith, who begat Esa, who begat Eoppa, who begat Ida. But Ida had twelve sons, Adda, Belric, Theodric, Ethelric, Theodhere, Osmer, and one queen, Bearnoch, Ealric. Ethelric begat Ethelfrid: the same is Aedlfred Flesaur. For he also had seven sons, Eanfrid, Oswald, Oswin, Oswy, Oswudu, Oslac, Offa. Oswy begat Alfrid, Elfwin, and Egfrid. Egfrid is he who made war against his cousin Brudei,

---

* V.R. By the holy bishop Amatheus.

† Here ends the Vatican MS. collated by Mr. Gunn.

‡ These titles are not part of the original work, but added in the MSS. by a later hand.

king of the Picts, and he fell therein with all the strength of his army, and the Picts with their king gained the victory; and the Saxons never again reduced the Picts so as to exact tribute from them. Since the time of this war it is called Gueithlin Garan.

But Oswy had two wives, Riemmelth, the daughter of Royth, son of Rum; and Eanfled, the daughter of Edwin, son of Alla.

The Genealogy Of The Kings Of Kent

58. Hengist begat Octa, who begat Ossa, who begat Eormenric, who begat Ethelbert, who begat Eadbald, who begat Ercombert, who begat Egbert.

The Origin Of The Kings Of East-Anglia

59. Woden begat Casser, who begat Titinon, who begat Trigil, who begat Rodmunt, who begat Rippa, who begat Guillem Guercha,* who was the first king of the East Angles. Guercha begat Uffa,

---

* Guercha is a distortion of the name of Uffa, or Wuffa, arising in the first instance from the pronunciation of the British writer; and in the next place from the error of the transcriber — Palgrave.

who begat Tytillus, who begat Eni, who begat Edric, who begat Aldwulf, who begat Elric.

The Genealogy Of The Mercians

Woden begat Guedolgeat, who begat Gueagon, who begat Guithleg, who begat Guerdmund, who begat Ossa, who begat Ongen, who begat Eamer, who begat Pubba.* This Pubba had twelve sons, of whom two are better known to me than the others, that is Penda and Eawa. Eadlit is the son of Pantha, Penda, son of Pubba, Ealbald, son of Alguing, son of Eawa, son of Penda, son of Pubba. Egfert, son of Offa, son of Thingferth, son of Enwulf, son of Ossulf, son of Eawa, son of Pubba.

The Kings of the Deiri

61. Woden begat Beldeg, Brond begat Siggar, who begat Sibald, who begat Zegulf, who begat Soemil, who first separated† Deur from Berneich (Deira from Bernicia.) Soemil begat Sguerthing, who begat Giulglis, who begat Ulfrea, who begat

---

* Or Wibba.

† V.R. Conquered.

Iffi, who begat Ulli, Edwin, Osfrid and Eanfrid. There were two sons of Edwin, who fell with him in battle at Meicen,* and the kingdom was never renewed in his family, because not one of his race escaped from that war; but all were slain with him by the army of Catguollaunus,† king of the Guendota. Oswy begat Egfrid, the same is Ailguin, who begat Oslach, sho begat Alhun, who begat Adlsing, who begat Echun, who begat Oslaph. Ida begat Eadric, who begat Ecgulf, who begat Leodwald, who begat Eata, the same is Glinmaur, who begat Eadbert and Egbert, who was the first bishop of their nation.

Ida, the son of Eoppa, possessed countries on the left-hand side of Britain, i.e. of the Humbrian sea, and reigned twelve years, and united‡ Dynguayth Guarth-Berneich.

62. Then Dutgirn at that time fought bravely against the nation of the Angles. At that time,

* Hatfield, in the West Riding of Yorkshire. See Bede's Eccles. Hist.
† Cadwalla, king of the Western Britons.
‡ V.R. United the castle, i.e. Dinguerin and Gurdbernech, which two countries were in one country, i.e. Deurabernech; Anglice Diera and Bernicia. Another MS. Built Dinguayrh Guarth Berneich.

Talhaiarn Cataguen* was famed for poetry, and Neirin, and Taliesin and Bluchbard, and Cian, who is called Guenith Guaut, were all famous at the same time in British poetry.

The great king, Mailcun,† reigned among the Britons, i.e. in the district of Guenedota, because his great-great-grandfather, Cunedda, with his twelve sons, had come before from the left-hand part, i.e. from the country which is called Manau Gustodin, one hundred and forty-six years before Mailcun reigned, and expelled the Scots with much slaughter from those countries, and they never returned again to inhabit them.

63. Adda, son of Ida, reigned eight years; Ethelric, son of Adda, reigned four years. Theodoric, son of Ida, reigned seven years. Freothwulf reigned six years. In whose time the kingdom of Kent, by the mission of Gregory, received baptism. Hussa reigned seven years. Against him fought four kings, Urien, and Ryderthen, and Guallauc, and Morcant. Theodoric fought bravely, together

---

* Talhaiarn was a descendant of Coel Godebog, and chaplain to Ambrosius.

† Better known as Maelgwn.

with his sons, against that Urien. But at that time sometimes the enemy and sometimes our countrymen were defeated, and he shut them up three days and three nights in the island of Metcaut; and whilst he was on an expedition he was murdered, at the instance of Morcant, out of envy, because he possessed so much superiority over all the kings in military science. Eadfered Flesaurs reigned twelve years in Bernicia, and twelve others in Deira, and gave to his wife Bebba, the town of Dynguaroy, which from her is called Bebbanburg.*

Edwin, son of Alla, reigned seventeen years, seized on Elmete, and expelled Cerdic, its king. Eanfled, his daughter, received baptism, on the twelfth day after Pentecost, with all her followers, both men and women. The following Easter Edwin himself received baptism, and twelve thousand of his subjects with him. If any one wishes to know who baptized them, it was Rum Map Urbgen:† he was engaged forty days in

---

* Bambrough. See Bede, iii. 6, and Sax. Chron. A.D. 547.

† See Bede's Eccles. Hist. From the share which Paulinus had in the conversion of the Northumbrian king, it has been inferred that he actually baptized him; but Nennius expressly states, that the holy sacrament was

baptizing all classes of the Saxons, and by his preaching many believed on Christ.

64. Oswald son of Ethelfrid, reigned nine years; the same is Oswald Llauiguin;* he slew Catgublaun (Cadwalla),† king of Guenedot,‡ in the battle of Catscaul,§ with much loss to his own army. Oswy, son of Ethelfrid, reigned twenty-eight years and six months. During his reign, there was a dreadful mortality among his subjects, when Catgualart (Cadwallader) was king among the Britons, succeeding his father, and he

---

administered by Rhun, the son of Urien. The Welsh name of Paulinus is Pawl Hen, or Polin Eagob.

* Llauiguin, means the 'fair,' or the 'bounteous hand.'

† This name has been variously written; Bede spells it Caedualla (Cadwalla); Nennius, Catgublaun; the Saxon Chronicle, Ceadwalla; and the Welsh writers, Cadwallon and Kalwallawn: and though the identity of the person may be clearly proved, it is necessary to observe these particulars to distinguish him from Cadwaladr, and from another Caedualla or Caedwalla, a king of the West Saxons; all of whom, as they lived within a short time of each other, have been frequently confounded together. — Rees's Welsh Saints.

‡ Gwynedd, North Wales.

§ Bede says at Denis's brook.

himself died amongst the rest.* He slew Penda in the field of Gai, and now took place the slaughter of Gai Campi, and the kings of the Britons, who went out with Penda on the expedition as far as the city of Judeu, were slain.

65. Then Oswy restored all the wealth, which was with him in the city, to Penda; who distributed it among the kings of the Britons, that is Atbert Judeu. But Catgabail alone, king of Guenedot, rising up in the night, escaped, together with his army, wherefore he was called Catgabail Catguommed. Egfrid, son of Oswy, reigned nine years. In his time the holy bishop Cuthbert died in the island of Medcaut.† It was he who made war against the Picts, and was by them slain.

Penda, son of Pybba, reigned ten years; he first separated the kingdom of Mercia from that of the North-men, and slew by treachery Anna, king of the East Anglians, and St. Oswald, king of the North Men. He fought the battle of Cocboy, in which fell Eawa, son of Pybba, his brother, king of

---

* The British chronicles assert that Cadwallader died at Rome, whilst Nennius would lead us to conclude that he perished in the pestilence at home.

† The isle of Farne.

the Mercians, and Oswald, king of the Northmen, and he gained the victory by diabolical agency. He was not baptized, and never believed in God.

66. From the beginning of the world to Constantinus and Rufus, are found to be five thousand six hundred and fifty-eight years.

Also from the two consuls, Rufus and Rubelius, to the consul Stilicho, are three hundred and seventy-three years.

Also from Stilicho to Valentinian, son of Placida, and the reign of Vortigern, are twenty-eight years.

And from the reign of Vortigern to the quarrel between Guitolinus and Ambrosius, are twelve years, which is Guoloppum, that is Catgwaloph.* Vortigern reigned in Britain when Theodosius and Valentinian were consuls, and in the fourth year of his reign the Saxons came to Britain, in the consulship of Felix and Taurus, in the four hundredth year from the incarnation of our Lord Jesus Christ.

---

* In Carmarthenshire. Perhaps the town now called Kidwelly.

From the year in which the Saxons came into Britain, and were received by Vortigern, to the time of Decius and Valerian, are sixty-nine years.

Cockatrice Books
Y diawl a'm llaw chwith

Published as part of the Wales in Europe series, celebrating the past and future of Wales as an independent nation.

The cockatrice is hatched from a cockerel's egg, and resembles a dragon the size and shape of a cockerel. The English word is derived from the Latin *calcatrix*, but in Welsh it is called *ceiliog neidr*: 'adder-cock.' Its touch, breath and glance are lethal.

There is a saying in Welsh, *Y ddraig goch ddyry cychwyn,* which means, 'The red dragon leads the way.' The cockatrice spits at your beery patriotism.

www.cockatrice-books.com

OWAIN GLYNDŴR
BY J. E. LLOYD

Published as part of the Wales in Europe series, celebrating the past and future of Wales as an independent nation

On 16th September 1400, Owain Glyndŵr, esquire, lawyer, land-owner, and descendant of the rulers of Wales, proclaimed himself Prince of Wales, thus beginning a period of effective independence and allegiance with France which lasted for more than ten years. This ground-breaking study by J. E. Lloyd, first published in 1930, considers his importance as guerrilla tactician, statesman and diplomat: the 'father of Welsh nationalism' who inspires Welsh thinkers and nation-builders to this day.

A BOOK OF THREE BIRDS
BY MORGAN LLWYD
translated with an introduction by Rob Mimpriss

Published as part of the Wales in Europe series, celebrating the past and future of Wales as an independent nation

Morgan Llwyd (1619-1659), the nephew of a professional soldier and magician, was a Roundhead, a millenialist, a chaplain in the army of Oliver Cromwell, and later a civil servant of the commonwealth in Wales.

His famous religious allegory, *A Book of Three Birds*, is considered the most important Welsh book of the Seventeenth Century, and an enduring masterpiece of Welsh prose. With its introduction reflecting on the political turmoils of our time, this new translation by Rob Mimpriss brings to life the pungency of Morgan Llwyd's writing, the richness of his religious and political thought, and the urgency of his drama and characterisation.

'Lucid, skilful, and above all, of enormous timely relevance.'

Jim Perrin

REASONING: TWENTY STORIES
by Rob Mimpriss

Reasoning is the first of three collections by Rob Mimpriss. It is followed by *For His Warriors* and *Prayer at the End.*

An old man tries to assess his guilt in the marriage his daughter has destroyed. A young man tries to understand why, in the same family, he should be both hated and loved. A seventeenth-century Puritan preacher and a Cardiff woman facing divorce unite in their call to 'know your innermost heart,' while a Romanian dissident under Ceaușescu and a Welsh-language activist find themselves outwardly liberated but inwardly still in chains.

'Rob Mimpriss could be described as a quiet writer with a loud voice. It's good to know he's planning ahead. I'll be listening for more.'

Michael Nobbs, gwales.com

FOR HIS WARRIORS: THIRTY STORIES
by Rob Mimpriss

For His Warriors is the second of three collections by Rob Mimpriss. It is preceded by *Reasoning* and followed by *Prayer at the End.*

A Welsh farmer's wife during the Second World War kills the landgirl her husband has taken as his lover. A leader of the Cornish-language revival commits her last act of protest the day Russian troops march into Berlin. A lonely man on the waterfront in Llandudno wonders whether he or his girlfriend will be first to die of Aids, and a bored man in a restaurant in Cardiff Bay invents a story of arrest and torture to amuse his petulant lover.

'Both humour and pity often arise from the characters' inability to understand themselves and those close to them. In suggesting both the truth and the self-deception Mimpriss not only engages our sympathy but makes us question our assumptions about ourselves.'

Caroline Clark, gwales.com

PRAYER AT THE END: TWENTY-THREE STORIES
by Rob Mimpriss

Prayer at the End is the third of three collections by Rob Mimpriss. It is preceded by *Reasoning* and *For His Warriors*.

A cigarette quenched in the Menai Strait makes a man vow to live a selfish life. The memory of an unborn twin makes a man regret the selfish life he has lived. An elderly shopkeeper befriends the teenagers outside his shop, and a lonely householder sets out to confront the trespassers on his land.

'In the most seemingly unremarkable of Rob Mimpriss's pieces there is a skill, and a mystery and elusiveness to that skill, which other short-story writers might envy. This is a masterful collection.'

Gee Williams

'heaving with loss, regret and familial bonds.'

Annexe Magazine

Made in the USA
Middletown, DE
18 August 2021

46249405R00071